05/08

Please return/renew this item
by last date shown.
Herefordshire Libraries

HEREFORDSHIRE
COUNCIL

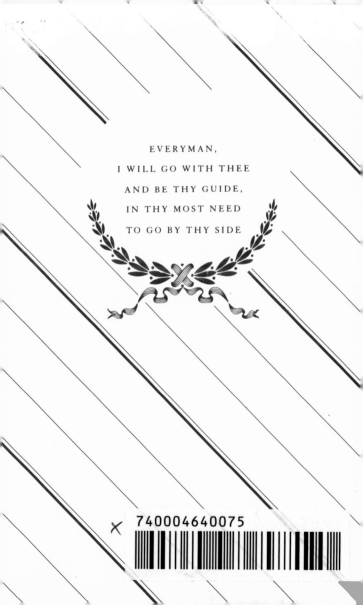

EVERYMAN,
I WILL GO WITH THEE
AND BE THY GUIDE,
IN THY MOST NEED
TO GO BY THY SIDE

సీతూ

EVERYMAN'S LIBRARY
POCKET POETS

SHELLEY

······················

POEMS

EVERYMAN'S LIBRARY
POCKET POETS

Alfred A. Knopf New York London Toronto

THIS IS A BORZOI BOOK
PUBLISHED BY ALFRED A. KNOPF

This selection first published in Everyman's Library, 1993
Copyright © 1993 by Everyman's Library

Tenth printing (US)

US website: www.randomhouse.com/everymans

ISBN 978-0-679-42909-8 (US)
LC 93-78335
978-1-85715-700-0 (UK)

A CIP catalogue record for this book is available from the British Library

Typography by Peter B. Willberg

Typeset in the UK by AccComputing, North Barrow, Somerset
Printed and bound in Germany by GGP Media GmbH, Pössneck

CONTENTS

LYRICAL
POEMS

LOVE'S PHILOSOPHY

The fountains mingle with the river
    And the rivers with the Ocean,
The winds of Heaven mix for ever
    With a sweet emotion;
Nothing in the world is single;
    All things by a law divine
In one spirit meet and mingle.
    Why not I with thine?—

See the mountains kiss high Heaven
    And the waves clasp one another;
No sister-flower would be forgiven
    If it disdained its brother;
And the sunlight clasps the earth
    And the moonbeams kiss the sea:
What is all this sweet work worth
    If thou kiss not me?

THE INDIAN SERENADE

I

I arise from dreams of thee
In the first sweet sleep of night.
When the winds are breathing low,
And the stars are shining bright:
I arise from dreams of thee,
And a spirit in my feet
Hath led me—who knows how?
To thy chamber window, Sweet!

II

The wandering airs they faint
On the dark, the silent stream—
The Champak odours fail
Like sweet thoughts in a dream;
The nightingale's complaint,
It dies upon her heart;—
As I must on thine,
Oh, belovèd as thou art!

III

Oh lift me from the grass!
I die! I faint! I fail!
Let thy love in kisses rain
On my lips and eyelids pale.
My cheek is cold and white, alas!
My heart beats loud and fast;—
Oh! press it to thine own again,
Where it will break at last.

WHEN PASSION'S TRANCE IS OVERPAST

When passion's trance is overpast,
If tenderness and truth could last
Or live, whilst all wild feelings keep
Some mortal slumber, dark and deep,
I should not weep, I should not weep!

It were enough to feel, to see
Thy soft eyes gazing tenderly,
And dream the rest—and burn and be
The secret food of fires unseen,
Could thou but be what thou hast been.

After the slumber of the year
The woodland violets reappear;
All things revive in field or grove
And sky and sea, but two, which move
And form all others—life and love.

LINES

The cold earth slept below,
    Above the cold sky shone;
And all around, with a chilling sound,
    From caves of ice and fields of snow,
    The breath of night like death did flow
      Beneath the sinking moon.

The wintry hedge was black,
    The green grass was not seen,
The birds did rest on the bare thorn's breast,
    Whose roots, beside the pathway track,
    Had bound their folds o'er many a crack
      Which the frost had made between.

Thine eyes glowed in the glare
        Of the moon's dying light;
As a fen-fire's beam on a sluggish stream
    Gleams dimly, so the moon shone there,
    And it yellowed the strings of thy raven hair,
        That shook in the wind of night.

The moon made thy lips pale, beloved—
        The wind made thy bosom chill—
The night did shed on thy dear head
    Its frozen dew, and thou didst lie
    Where the bitter breath of the naked sky
        Might visit thee at will.

Fragment: ROSE LEAVES,
WHEN THE ROSE IS DEAD

Rose leaves, when the rose is dead,
Are heaped for the beloved's bed,
And so thy thoughts, when thou art gone,
Love itself shall slumber on.

Music, when soft voices die,
Vibrates in the memory,—
Odours, when sweet violets sicken,
Live within the sense they quicken—

O WORLD, O LIFE, O TIME

O World, O Life, O Time,
On whose last steps I climb,
Trembling at that where I had stood before—
When will return the glory of your prime?
No more, O never more!

Out of the day and night
A joy has taken flight—
Fresh spring and summer, and winter hoar,
Move my faint heart with grief, but with delight
No more, O never more!

THE FLOWER THAT SMILES TODAY

The flower that smiles today
   Tomorrow dies;
All that we wish to stay
   Tempts and then flies;
What is this world's delight?
Lightning, that mocks the night,
   Brief even as bright.—

Virtue, how frail it is!—
   Friendship, how rare!—
Love, how it sells poor bliss
   For proud despair!
But these, though soon they fall,
Survive their joy, and all
   Which ours we call.—

Whilst skies are blue and bright,
   Whilst flowers are gay,
Whilst eyes that change ere night
   Make glad the day;
Whilst yet the calm hours creep,
Dream thou—and from thy sleep
   Then wake to weep.

Fragment: TO THE MOON

   Art thou pale for weariness
Of climbing Heaven, and gazing on the earth,
   Wandering companionless
Among the stars that have a different birth,—
And ever changing, like a joyless eye
That finds no object worth its constancy?

Fragment: THE WANING MOON

And like a dying lady, lean and pale,
Who totters forth, wrapped in a gauzy veil,
Out of her chamber, led by the insane
And feeble wanderings of her fading brain,
The moon arose up in the murky East,
A white and shapeless mass—

THE CLOUD

I bring fresh showers for the thirsting flowers,
    From the seas and the streams;
I bear light shade for the leaves when laid
    In their noonday dreams.
From my wings are shaken the dews that waken
    The sweet buds every one,
When rocked to rest on their mother's breast,
    As she dances about the sun.
I wield the flail of the lashing hail,
    And whiten the green plains under,
And then again I dissolve it in rain,
    And laugh as I pass in thunder.

I sift the snow on the mountains below,
    And their great pines groan aghast;
And all the night 'tis my pillow white,
    While I sleep in the arms of the blast.
Sublime on the towers of my skiey bowers,
    Lightning my pilot sits;
In a cavern under is fettered the thunder,
    It struggles and howls at fits;
Over earth and ocean, with gentle motion,
    This pilot is guiding me,
Lured by the love of the genii that move
    In the depths of the purple sea;

Over the rills, and the crags, and the hills,
    Over the lakes and the plains,
Wherever he dream, under mountain or stream,
    The Spirit he loves remains;
And I all the while bask in Heaven's blue smile,
    Whilst he is dissolving in rains.

The sanguine Sunrise, with his meteor eyes,
    And his burning plumes outspread,
Leaps on the back of my sailing rack,
    When the morning star shines dead;
As on the jag of a mountain crag,
    Which an earthquake rocks and swings,
An eagle alit one moment may sit
    In the light of its golden wings.
And when Sunset may breathe, from the lit sea
    Its ardours of rest and of love,   [beneath,
And the crimson pall of eve may fall
    From the depth of Heaven above,
With wings folded I rest, on mine aëry nest,
    As still as a brooding dove.

That orbèd maiden with white fire laden,
    Whom mortals call the Moon,
Glides glimmering o'er my fleece-like floor,
    By the midnight breezes strewn;
And wherever the beat of her unseen feet,

Which only the angels hear,
May have broken the woof of my tent's thin roof,
    The stars peep behind her and peer;
And I laugh to see them whirl and flee,
    Like a swarm of golden bees,
When I widen the rent in my wind-built tent,
    Till the calm rivers, lakes, and seas,
Like strips of the sky fallen through me on high,
    Are each paved with the moon and these.

I bind the Sun's throne with a burning zone,
    And the Moon's with a girdle of pearl;
The volcanoes are dim, and the stars reel and swim,
    When the whirlwinds my banner unfurl.
From cape to cape, with a bridge-like shape,
    Over a torrent sea,
Sunbeam-proof, I hang like a roof,—
    The mountains its columns be.
The triumphal arch through which I march
    With hurricane, fire, and snow,
When the Powers of the air are chained to my chair,
    Is the million-coloured bow;
The sphere-fire above its soft colours wove,
    While the moist Earth was laughing below.

I am the daughter of Earth and Water,
    And the nursling of the Sky;

I pass through the pores of the ocean and shores;
    I change, but I cannot die.
For after the rain when with never a stain
    The pavilion of Heaven is bare,
And the winds and sunbeams with their convex gleams
    Build up the blue dome of air,
I silently laugh at my own cenotaph,
    And out of the caverns of rain,
Like a child from the womb, like a ghost from the
    I arise and unbuild it again.   [tomb,

Two Songs for *Midas*
SONG OF APOLLO

The sleepless Hours who watch me as I lie
   Curtained with star-enwoven tapestries
From the broad moonlight of the open sky,
   Fanning the busy dreams from my dim eyes,—
Waken me when their mother, the grey Dawn,
Tells them that dreams and that the moon is gone.

Then I arise; and climbing Heaven's blue dome,
   I walk over the mountains and the waves,
Leaving my robe upon the ocean foam;
   My footsteps pave the clouds with fire; the caves
Are filled with my bright presence, and the air
Leaves the green Earth to my embraces bare.

The sunbeams are my shafts with which I kill
   Deceit, that loves the night and fears the day;
All men who do, or even imagine ill
   Fly me; and from the glory of my ray
Good minds and open actions take new might,
Until diminished by the reign of night.

I feed the clouds, the rainbows and the flowers
   With their aethereal colours; the moon's globe
And the pure stars in their eternal bowers
   Are cinctured with my power as with a robe;
Whatever lamps on Earth or Heaven may shine
Are portions of one spirit; which is mine.

I stand at noon upon the peak of Heaven;
   Then with unwilling steps, I linger down
Into the clouds of the Atlantic even;
   For grief that I depart they weep and frown—
What look is more delightful, than the smile
With which I soothe them from the Western isle?

I am the eye with which the Universe
   Beholds itself, and knows it is divine;
All harmony of instrument and verse,
   All prophecy and medicine are mine,
All light of art or nature:—to my song
Victory and praise, in its own right, belong.

SONG OF PAN

From the forests and highlands
   We come, we come,
From the river-girt islands
   Where loud waves were dumb,
    Listening my sweet pipings.
      The wind in the reeds and the rushes,
      The bees on the bells of thyme,
      The birds in the myrtle bushes,
      The cicadæ above in the lime,
        And the lizards below in the grass,
Were silent as even old Tmolus was,
      Listening my sweet pipings.

Liquid Peneus was flowing,
   And all dark Tempe lay
In Pelion's shadow, outgrowing
   The light of the dying day,
    Speeded with my sweet pipings.
      The sileni and sylvans and fauns
      And the nymphs of the woods and the waves
      To the edge of the moist river-lawns
      And the brink of the dewy caves,
        And all that did then attend and follow
Were as silent for love, as you now, Apollo,
      For envy of my sweet pipings.

I sang of the dancing stars,
    I sang of the dædal Earth,
And of Heaven, and the giant wars,
    And Love and Death and Birth;
       And then I changed my pipings,
       Singing how, down the vales of Mænalus
       I pursued a maiden and clasped a reed.
       Gods and men, we are all deluded thus!—
       It breaks on our bosom and then we bleed.
       They wept as I think both ye now would,
If envy or age had not frozen your blood,
       At the sorrow of my sweet pipings.

TO NIGHT

Swiftly walk o'er the western wave,
    Spirit of Night!
Out of the misty eastern cave
Where, all the long and lone daylight
Thou wovest dreams of joy and fear,
Which make thee terrible and dear,
    Swift be thy flight!

Wrap thy form in a mantle grey,
    Star-inwrought!
Blind with thine hair the eyes of Day,
Kiss her until she be wearied out—
Then wander o'er city and sea and land,
Touching all with thine opiate wand—
    Come, long-sought!

When I arose and saw the dawn
    I sighed for thee;
When light rode high, and the dew was gone,
And noon lay heavy on flower and tree,
And the weary Day turned to his rest,
Lingering like an unloved guest,
    I sighed for thee.

Thy brother Death came, and cried,
　　'Wouldst thou me?'
Thy sweet child Sleep, the filmy-eyed,
Murmured like a noontide bee,
'Shall I nestle near thy side?
Wouldst thou me?' and I replied,
　　'No, not thee!'

Death will come when thou art dead,
　　Soon, too soon—
Sleep will come when thou art fled;
Of neither would I ask the boon
I ask of thee, belovèd Night—
Swift be thine approaching flight,
　　Come soon, soon!

ODE TO THE WEST WIND

1. O wild West Wind, thou breath of Autumn's being,
   Thou, from whose unseen presence the leaves dead
   Are driven, like ghosts from an enchanter fleeing,

   Yellow, and black, and pale, and hectic red,
   Pestilence-stricken multitudes: O thou,
   Who chariotest to their dark wintry bed

   The wingèd seeds, where they lie cold and low,
   Each like a corpse within its grave, until
   Thine azure sister of the Spring shall blow

   Her clarion o'er the dreaming earth, and fill
   (Driving sweet buds like flocks to feed in air)
   With living hues and odours plain and hill:

   Wild Spirit, which art moving everywhere;
   Destroyer and Preserver; hear, O hear!

2. Thou on whose stream, 'mid the steep sky's
                          [commotion,
  Loose clouds like Earth's decaying leaves are shed,
  Shook from the tangled boughs of Heaven and Ocean,

  Angels of rain and lightning: there are spread
  On the blue surface of thine airy surge,
  Like the bright hair uplifted from the head

  Of some fierce Mænad, even from the dim verge
  Of the horizon to the zenith's height,
  The locks of the approaching storm. Thou dirge

  Of the dying year, to which this closing night
  Will be the dome of a vast sepulchre
  Vaulted with all thy congregated might

  Of vapours, from whose solid atmosphere
  Black rain, and fire, and hail will burst: O hear!

3. Thou who didst waken from his summer dreams
   The blue Mediterranean, where he lay,
   Lulled by the coil of his crystalline streams,

   Beside a pumice isle in Baiæ's bay,
   And saw in sleep old palaces and towers
   Quivering within the wave's intenser day,

   All overgrown with azure moss and flowers
   So sweet, the sense faints picturing them! Thou
   For whose path the Atlantic's level powers

   Cleave themselves into chasms, while far below
   The sea-blooms and the oozy woods which wear
   The sapless foliage of the ocean, know

   Thy voice, and suddenly grow grey with fear,
   And tremble and despoil themselves: O hear!

4. If I were a dead leaf thou mightest bear;
   If I were a swift cloud to fly with thee;
   A wave to pant beneath thy power, and share

   The impulse of thy strength, only less free
   Than thou, O Uncontrollable! If even
   I were as in my boyhood, and could be

   The comrade of thy wanderings over Heaven,
   As then, when to outstrip thy skiey speed
   Scarce seemed a vision; I would ne'er have striven

   As thus with thee in prayer in my sore need.
   Oh! lift me as a wave, a leaf, a cloud!
   I fall upon the thorns of life! I bleed!

   A heavy weight of hours has chained and bowed
   One too like thee: tameless, and swift, and proud.

5. Make me thy lyre, even as the forest is:
   What if my leaves are falling like its own!
   The tumult of thy mighty harmonies

   Will take from both a deep, autumnal tone,
   Sweet though in sadness. Be thou, Spirit fierce,
   My spirit! Be thou me, impetuous one!

   Drive my dead thoughts over the universe
   Like withered leaves to quicken a new birth!
   And, by the incantation of this verse,

   Scatter, as from an unextinguished hearth
   Ashes and sparks, my words among mankind!
   Be through my lips to unawakened Earth

   The trumpet of a prophecy! O Wind,
   If Winter comes, can Spring be far behind?

TO A SKY-LARK

Hail to thee, blithe Spirit!
    Bird thou never wert,
That from Heaven, or near it,
    Pourest thy full heart
In profuse strains of unpremeditated art.

Higher still and higher
    From the earth thou springest
Like a cloud of fire;
    The blue deep thou wingest,
And singing still dost soar, and soaring ever singest.

In the golden lightning
    Of the sunken Sun,
O'er which clouds are bright'ning,
    Thou dost float and run;
Like an unbodied joy whose race is just begun.

The pale purple even
    Melts around thy flight;
Like a star of Heaven
    In the broad day-light
Thou art unseen,—but yet I hear thy shrill delight,

Keen as are the arrows
    Of that silver sphere
Whose intense lamp narrows
    In the white dawn clear,
Until we hardly see—we feel that it is there.

All the earth and air
    With thy voice is loud,
As when night is bare
    From one lonely cloud
The moon rains out her beams, and Heaven is
                                    ⌈overflowed.
What thou art we know not;
    What is most like thee?
From rainbow clouds there flow not
    Drops so bright to see,
As from thy presence showers a rain of melody.

Like a Poet hidden
    In the light of thought,
Singing hymns unbidden
    Till the world is wrought
To sympathy with hopes and fears it heeded not:

Like a high-born maiden
    In a palace tower,
Soothing her love-laden
    Soul in secret hour
With music sweet as love, which overflows her bower:

Like a glow-worm golden
    In a dell of dew,
Scattering unbeholden
    Its aërial hue
Among the flowers and grass which screen it from the
                                    [view:

Like a rose embowered
    In its own green leaves,
By warm winds deflowered,
    Till the scent it gives
Makes faint with too much sweet those heavy-wingèd
                                    [thieves:

Sound of vernal showers
    On the twinkling grass,
Rain-awakened flowers,
    All that ever was
Joyous and clear and fresh, thy music doth surpass.

Teach us, Sprite or Bird,
    What sweet thoughts are thine;
I have never heard
    Praise of love or wine
That panted forth a flood of rapture so divine:

Chorus Hymenæal
    Or triumphal chaunt
Matched with thine, would be all
    But an empty vaunt,
A thing wherein we feel there is some hidden want.

What objects are the fountains
    Of thy happy strain?
What fields or waves or mountains?
    What shapes of sky or plain?
What love of thine own kind? what ignorance of pain?

With thy clear keen joyance
    Languor cannot be—
Shadow of annoyance
    Never came near thee:
Thou lovest—but ne'er knew love's sad satiety.

Waking or asleep,
 Thou of death must deem
Things more true and deep
 Than we mortals dream,
Or how could thy notes flow in such a crystal stream?

We look before and after
 And pine for what is not:
Our sincerest laughter
 With some pain is fraught;
Our sweetest songs are those that tell of saddest
          [thought.

Yet if we could scorn
 Hate and pride and fear;
If we were things born
 Not to shed a tear,
I know not how thy joy we ever should come near.

Better than all measures
 Of delightful sound—
Better than all treasures
 That in books are found—
Thy skill to poet were, thou scorner of the ground!

Teach me half the gladness
    That thy brain must know,
Such harmonious madness
    From my lips would flow,
The world should listen then—as I am listening now.

VERSES WRITTEN ON RECEIVING A CELANDINE IN A LETTER FROM ENGLAND

I thought of thee, fair Celandine,
  As of a flower aery blue
Yet small—thy leaves methought were wet
  With the light of morning dew.
In the same glen thy star did shine
As the primrose and the violet,
And the wild briar bent over thee
And the woodland brook danced under thee.

Lovely thou wert in thine own glen
  Ere thou didst dwell in song or story;
Ere the moonlight of a Poet's mind
  Had arrayed thee with the glory
Whose fountains are the hearts of men—
Many a thing of vital kind
Had fed and sheltered under thee,
Had nourished their thoughts near to thee.

Yes, gentle flower in thy recess,
    None might a sweeter aspect wear,
Thy young bud drooped so gracefully,
    Thou wert so very fair,—
Among the fairest, ere the stress
Of exile, death and injury,
Thus withering and deforming thee,
Had made a mournful type of thee,

A type of that when I and thou
    Are thus familiar, Celandine—
A deathless Poet whose young prime
    Was as serene as thine!
But he is changed and withered now,
Fallen on a cold and evil time;
His heart is gone—his fame is dim,
And Infamy sits mocking him.

Celandine! Thou art pale and dead,
    Changed from thy fresh and woodland state;
Oh! that thy bard were cold, but he
    Has lived too long and late.
Would he were in an honoured grave!
But that, men say, now must not be,
Since he for impious gold could sell
The love of those who loved him well.

That he, with all hope else of good
    Should be thus transitory,
I marvel not; but that his lays
    Have spared not their own glory—
That blood, even the foul god of blood
With most inexpiable praise,
Freedom and truth left desolate,
He has been bought to celebrate!

They were his hopes which he doth scorn;
    They were his foes the fight that won;
That sanction and that condemnation
    Are now forever gone.
They need them not! Truth may not mourn
That with a liar's inspiration
Her majesty he did disown
Ere he could overlive his own.

They need them not, for Liberty,
    Justice and philosophic truth
From his divine and simple song
    Shall draw immortal youth,
When he and thou shall cease to be
Or be some other thing,—so long
As men may breathe or flowers may blossom
O'er the wide earth's maternal bosom.

The stem whence thou wert disunited
   Since thy poor self was banished hither,
Now, by that priest of Nature's care
   Who sent thee forth to wither,
His window with its blooms has lighted,
And I shall see thy brethren there.
And each, like thee, will aye betoken
Love sold, hope dead, and honour broken.

SONG

Rarely, rarely, comest thou,
    Spirit of Delight!
Wherefore hast thou left me now
    Many a day and night?
Many a weary night and day
'Tis since thou art fled away.

How shall ever one like me
    Win thee back again?
With the joyous and the free
    Thou wilt scoff at pain.
Spirit false! that hast forgot
All but those who need thee not.

As a lizard with the shade
    Of a trembling leaf,
Thou with sorrow art dismayed;
    Even the sighs of grief
Reproach thee, that thou art not near,
And reproach thou wilt not hear.

Let me set my mournful ditty
   To a merry measure;
Thou wilt never come for pity,
   Thou wilt come for pleasure;
Pity then will cut away
Those cruel wings, and thou wilt stay.

I love all that thou lovest,
   Spirit of Delight!
The fresh Earth in new leaves dressed,
   And the starry night;
Autumn evening, and the morn
When the golden mists are born.

I love snow, and all the forms
   Of the radiant frost;
I love waves and winds and storms—
   Every thing almost
Which is Nature's, and may be
Untainted by man's misery.

I love tranquil solitude,
  And such society
As is quiet, wise and good;
  Between thee and me
What difference?—but thou dost possess
The things I seek, not love them less.

I love Love—though he has wings,
  And like light can flee—
But above all other things,
  Spirit, I love thee—
Thou art Love and Life! O come,
Make once more my heart thy home.

STANZAS WRITTEN IN DEJECTION
December 1818, near Naples

The Sun is warm, the sky is clear,
The waves are dancing fast and bright,
Blue isles and snowy mountains wear
The purple noon's transparent might,
The breath of the moist earth is light
Around its unexpanded buds;
Like many a voice of one delight
The winds, the birds, the Ocean-floods;
The City's voice itself is soft, like Solitude's.

I see the Deep's untrampled floor
With green and purple seaweeds strown,
I see the waves upon the shore
Like light dissolved in star-showers, thrown;
I sit upon the sands alone;
The lightning of the noontide Ocean
Is flashing round me, and a tone
Arises from its measured motion,
How sweet! did any heart now share in my emotion.

Alas, I have nor hope nor health,
Nor peace within nor calm around,
Nor that content surpassing wealth
The sage in meditation found,
And walked with inward glory crowned;
Nor fame nor power nor love nor leisure—
Others I see whom these surround,
Smiling they live and call life pleasure:
To me that cup has been dealt in another measure.

Yet now despair itself is mild,
Even as the winds and waters are;
I could lie down like a tired child
And weep away the life of care
Which I have borne and yet must bear,
Till Death like Sleep might steal on me,
And I might feel in the warm air
My cheek grow cold, and hear the Sea
Breathe o'er my dying brain its last monotony.

Some might lament that I were cold,
As I, when this sweet day is gone,
Which my lost heart, too soon grown old,
Insults with this untimely moan—
They might lament,—for I am one
Whom men love not, and yet regret;
Unlike this day, which, when the Sun
Shall on its stainless glory set,
Will linger, though enjoyed, like joy in memory yet.

THE AZIOLA

'Do you not hear the aziola cry?
Methinks she must be nigh—'
    Said Mary as we sate
In dusk, ere stars were lit or candles brought—
    And I who thought
This Aziola was some tedious woman
Asked, 'Who is Aziola?'—how elate
I felt to know that it was nothing human,
No mockery of myself to fear or hate!
    And Mary saw my soul,
And laughed and said—'Disquiet yourself not,
    'Tis nothing but a little downy owl.'

Sad aziola, many an eventide
    Thy music I had heard
By wood and stream, meadow and mountainside,
And fields and marshes wide,
Such as nor voice, nor lute, nor wind, nor bird
    The soul ever stirred—
Unlike and far sweeter than them all.
Sad aziola, from that moment I
Loved thee and thy sad cry.

TO JANE

The keen stars were twinkling
And the fair moon was rising among them,
    Dear Jane.
The guitar was tinkling
But the notes were not sweet till you sung them
    Again.—

As the moon's soft splendour
O'er the faint cold starlight of Heaven
    Is thrown—
So your voice most tender
To the strings without soul had then given
    Its own.

The stars will awaken,
Though the moon sleep a full hour later,
    Tonight;
  No leaf will be shaken
While the dews of your melody scatter
    Delight.

Though the sound overpowers,
Sing again, with your dear voice revealing
    A tone
Of some world far from ours,
Where music and moonlight and feeling
    Are one.

From HELLAS: TWO CHORUSES

1.   Worlds on worlds are rolling ever
      From creation to decay,
  Like the bubbles on a river
      Sparkling, bursting, borne away.
        But *they* are still immortal
         Who, through Birth's orient portal
  And Death's dark chasm hurrying to and fro,
      Clothe their unceasing flight
      In the brief dust and light
Gathered around their chariots as they go;
      New shapes they still may weave,
      New gods, new laws receive,
Bright or dim are they as the robes they last
    On Death's bare ribs had cast.

A Power from the unknown God,
    A Promethean conqueror, came;
Like a triumphal path he trod
    The thorns of death and shame.
        A mortal shape to him
        Was like the vapour dim
Which the orient planet animates with light;
        Hell, Sin, and Slavery came
        Like bloodhounds mild and tame,
Nor preyed, until their Lord had taken flight;
        The moon of Mahomet
        Arose, and it shall set
While blazoned as on Heaven's immortal noon
    The cross leads generations on.

Swift as the radiant shapes of sleep
　　From one whose dreams are Paradise
Fly, when the fond wretch wakes to weep
　　And Day peers forth with her blank eyes,
　　　　So fleet, so faint, so fair,
　　　　The Powers of earth and air
Fled from the folding-star of Bethlehem:
　　　　Apollo, Pan, and Love,
　　　　And even Olympian Jove
Grew weak, for killing Truth had glared on them;
　　　　Our hills and seas and streams,
　　　　Dispeopled of their dreams,
Their waters turned to blood, their dew to tears,
　　　　Wailed for the golden years.

2.   The world's great age begins anew,
      The golden years return,
    The earth doth like a snake renew
      Her winter weeds outworn;
Heaven smiles, and faiths and empires gleam
Like wrecks of a dissolving dream.

    A brighter Hellas rears its mountains
      From waves serener far,
    A new Peneus rolls his fountains
      Against the morning-star;
Where fairer Tempes bloom, there sleep
Young Cyclads on a sunnier deep.

    A loftier Argo cleaves the main
      Fraught with a later prize;
    Another Orpheus sings again,
      And loves, and weeps, and dies;
A new Ulysses leaves once more
Calypso for his native shore.

    O, write no more the tale of Troy,
      If earth Death's scroll must be!
    Nor mix with Laian rage the joy
      Which dawns upon the free;
Although a subtler Sphinx renew
Riddles of death Thebes never knew.

Another Athens shall arise,
    And to remoter time
Bequeath, like sunset to the skies,
    The splendour of its prime;
And leave, if nought so bright may live,
All earth can take or Heaven can give.

    Saturn and Love their long repose
       Shall burst, more bright and good
Than all who fell, than One who rose,
       Than many unsubdued;
Not gold, not blood, their altar dowers,
But votive tears and symbol flowers.

    O cease! must hate and death return?
       Cease! must men kill and die?
    Cease! drain not to its dregs the urn
       Of bitter prophecy.
The world is weary of the past,
O might it die or rest at last!

OZYMANDIAS

I met a traveller from an antique land
Who said: 'Two vast and trunkless legs of stone
Stand in the desert. Near them, on the sand,
Half sunk, a shattered visage lies, whose frown,
And wrinkled lip, and sneer of cold command,
Tell that its sculptor well those passions read
Which yet survive, stamped on these lifeless things,
The hand that mocked them and the heart that fed;
And on the pedestal these words appear:
"My name is Ozymandias, king of kings:
Look on my works, ye Mighty, and despair!"
Nothing beside remains. Round the decay
Of that colossal wreck, boundless and bare
The lone and level sands stretch far away.'

POLITICAL
AND
PHILOSOPHICAL
POEMS

ENGLAND IN 1819

An old, mad, blind, despised and dying King;
Princes, the dregs of their dull race, who flow
Through public scorn,—mud from a muddy spring;
Rulers who neither see nor feel nor know,
But leechlike to their fainting Country cling
Till they drop, blind in blood, without a blow;
A people starved and stabbed on the untilled field;
An army whom liberticide and prey
Makes as a two-edged sword to all who wield;
Golden and sanguine laws which tempt and slay;
Religion Christless, Godless, a book sealed;
A senate, Time's worst statute, unrepealed,—
Are graves from which a glorious Phantom may
Burst, to illumine our tempestuous day.

SONG TO THE MEN OF ENGLAND

I

Men of England, wherefore plough
For the lords who lay ye low?
Wherefore weave with toil and care
The rich robes your tyrants wear?

II

Wherefore feed, and clothe, and save,
From the cradle to the grave,
Those ungrateful drones who would
Drain your sweat—nay, drink your blood?

III

Wherefore, Bees of England, forge
Many a weapon, chain, and scourge,
That these stingless drones may spoil
The forced produce of your toil?

IV

Have ye leisure, comfort, calm,
Shelter, food, love's gentle balm?
Or what is it ye buy so dear
With your pain and with your fear?

V

The seed ye sow, another reaps;
The wealth ye find, another keeps;
The robes ye weave, another wears;
The arms ye forge, another bears.

VI

Sow seed,—but let no tyrant reap;
Find wealth,—let no imposter heap;
Weave robes,—let not the idle wear;
Forge arms,—in your defence to bear.

VII

Shrink to your cellars, holes, and cells;
In halls ye deck another dwells.
Why shake the chains ye wrought? Ye see
The steel ye tempered glance on ye.

VIII

With plough and spade, and hoe and loom,
Trace your grave, and build your tomb,
And weave your winding-sheet, till fair
England be your sepulchre.

TO THE LORD CHANCELLOR

1. Thy country's curse is on thee, darkest crest
    Of that foul, knotted, many-headed worm
   Which rends our Mother's bosom—Priestly Pest!
    Masked Resurrection of a buried Form!

2. Thy country's curse is on thee! Justice sold,
    Truth trampled, Nature's landmarks overthrown,
   And heaps of fraud-accumulated gold
    Plead, loud as thunder, at Destruction's throne.

3. And, whilst that sure slow Angel which aye stands
    Watching the beck of Mutability
   Delays to execute her high commands,
    And, though a nation weeps, spares thine and thee,

4. O, let a father's curse be on thy soul,
    And let a daughter's hope be on thy tomb;
   Be both, on thy grey head, a leaden cowl
    To weigh thee down to thy approaching doom!

5. I curse thee—by a parent's outraged love,
        By hopes long cherished and too lately lost,
    By gentle feelings thou couldst never prove,
        By griefs which thy stern nature never crossed;

6. By those infantine smiles of happy light,
        Which were a fire within a stranger's hearth,
    Quenched even when kindled, in untimely night
        Hiding the promise of a lovely birth;

7. By those unpractised accents of young speech,
        Which he who is a father thought to frame
    To gentlest lore, such as the wisest teach—
        Thou strike the lyre of mind!—oh, grief and shame!

8. By all the happy see in children's growth—
        That undeveloped flower of budding years—
    Sweetness and sadness interwoven both,
        Source of the sweetest hopes and saddest fears;

9. By all the days, under a hireling's care,
    Of dull constraint and bitter heaviness,—
   O wretched ye if ever any were,—
    Sadder than orphans, yet not fatherless;

10. By the false cant which on their innocent lips
    Must hang like poison on an opening bloom;
   By the dark creeds which cover with eclipse
    Their pathway from the cradle to the tomb;

11. By thy most impious Hell, and all its terror;
    By all the grief, the madness, and the guilt
   Of thine impostures, which must be their error—
    That sand on which thy crumbling Power is built;

12. By thy complicity with lust and hate—
    Thy thirst for tears—thy hunger after gold—
   The ready frauds which ever on thee wait—
    The servile arts in which thou hast grown old;

13. By thy most killing sneer, and by thy smile,
     By all the snares and nets of thy black den;
   And—for thou canst outweep the crocodile—
     By thy false tears—those millstones braining men—

14. By all the hate which checks a father's love—
     By all the scorn which kills a father's care—
   By those most impious hands which dared remove
     Nature's high bounds—by thee—and by despair—

15. Yes, the despair which bids a father groan,
     And cry, 'My children are no longer mine—
   The blood within those veins may be mine own,
     But, Tyrant, their polluted souls are thine!'—

16. I curse thee, though I hate thee not.—O slave!
     If thou couldst quench the earth-consuming Hell
   Of which thou art a daemon, on thy grave
     This curse should be a blessing. Fare thee well!

THE MASK OF ANARCHY
Written on the Occasion of the
Massacre at Manchester

As I lay asleep in Italy
There came a voice from over the Sea,
And with great power it forth led me
To walk in the Visions of Poesy.

I met Murder on the way—
He had a mask like Castlereagh,
Very smooth he looked, yet grim;
Seven bloodhounds followed him:

All were fat; and well they might
Be in admirable plight,
For one by one, and two by two,
He tossed them human hearts to chew
Which from his wide cloak he drew.

Next came Fraud, and he had on,
Like Eldon, an ermined gown;
His big tears, for he wept well,
Turned to mill-stones as they fell,

And the little children who
Round his feet played to and fro,
Thinking every tear a gem,
Had their brains knocked out by them.

Clothed with the Bible, as with light,
And the shadows of the night,
Like Sidmouth next, Hypocrisy
On a crocodile rode by.

And many more Destructions played
In this ghastly masquerade,
All disguised, even to the eyes,
Like Bishops, lawyers, peers or spies.

Last came Anarchy: he rode
On a white horse, splashed with blood;
He was pale even to the lips,
Like Death in the Apocalypse.

And he wore a kingly crown;
And in his grasp a sceptre shone;
On his brow this mark I saw—
'I AM GOD AND KING AND LAW.'

With a pace stately and fast,
Over English land he passed,
Trampling to a mire of blood
The adoring multitude.

And a mighty troop around,
With their trampling shook the ground,
Waving each a bloody sword,
For the service of their Lord;

And with glorious triumph, they
Rode through England proud and gay,
Drunk as with intoxication
Of the wine of desolation.

O'er fields and towns, from sea to sea,
Passed that Pageant swift and free,
Tearing up and trampling down
Till they came to London town;

And each dweller, panic-stricken,
Felt his heart with terror sicken
Hearing the tempestuous cry
Of the triumph of Anarchy.

For with pomp to meet him came
Clothed in arms like blood and flame
The hired Murderers, who did sing
'Thou art God and Law and King.

'We have waited weak and lone
For thy coming, Mighty One!
Our purses are empty, our swords are cold,
Give us glory and blood and gold.'

Lawyers and priests, a motley crowd,
To the Earth their pale brows bowed,
Like a bad prayer not overloud
Whispering—'Thou art Law and God.'

Then all cried with one accord
'Thou art King and God and Lord;
Anarchy, to Thee we bow,
Be Thy name made holy now!'

And Anarchy, the Skeleton,
Bowed and grinned to every one,
As well as if his education
Had cost ten millions to the Nation.

For he knew the Palaces
Of our Kings were rightly his;
His the sceptre, crown, and globe,
And the gold-inwoven robe.

So he sent his slaves before
To seize upon the Bank and Tower,
And was proceeding with intent
To meet his pensioned Parliament

When One fled past, a Maniac maid,
And her name was Hope, she said:
But she looked more like Despair,
And she cried out in the air—

'My father Time is weak and grey
With waiting for a better day—
See how idiot-like he stands
Fumbling with his palsied hands!

'He has had child after child
And the dust of death is piled
Over every one but me—
Misery, O Misery!'

Then she lay down in the street
Right before the horses' feet,
Expecting with a patient eye
Murder, Fraud and Anarchy,

When between her and her foes
A mist, a light, an image rose,
Small at first, and weak and frail
Like the vapour of a vale,

Till as clouds grow on the blast
Like tower-crowned giants striding fast,
And glare with lightnings as they fly
And speak in thunder to the sky,

It grew—a Shape arrayed in mail
Brighter than the viper's scale,
And upborne on wings whose grain
Was as the light of sunny rain.

On its helm seen far away
A planet, like the Morning's lay;
And those plumes its light rained through
Like a shower of crimson dew;

With step as soft as wind it passed
O'er the heads of men—so fast
That they knew the presence there
And looked—but all was empty air.

As flowers beneath May's footstep waken,
As stars from Night's loose hair are shaken,
As waves arise when loud winds call,
Thoughts sprung where'er that step did fall.

And the prostrate multitude
Looked—and ankle-deep in blood
Hope, that maiden most serene,
Was walking with a quiet mien,

And Anarchy, the ghastly birth,
Lay dead earth upon the earth—
The Horse of Death tameless as wind
Fled, and with his hoofs did grind
To dust the murderers thronged behind.

A rushing light of clouds and splendour,
A sense awakening and yet tender
Was heard and felt—and at its close
These words of joy and fear arose

As if their own indignant Earth
Which gave the Sons of England birth
Had felt their blood upon her brow,
And shuddering with a mother's throe

Had turned every drop of blood
By which her face had been bedewed
To an accent unwithstood—
As if her heart cried out aloud:

'Men of England, Heirs of Glory,
Heroes of unwritten Story,
Nurslings of one mighty Mother,
Hopes of her and one another,

'Rise like Lions after slumber
In unvanquishable number,
Shake your chains to Earth like dew
Which in sleep had fallen on you—
Ye are many—they are few.

'What is Freedom?—ye can tell
That which slavery is, too well—
For its very name has grown
To an echo of your own.

' 'Tis to work and have such pay
As just keeps life from day to day
In your limbs, as in a cell
For the tyrants' use to dwell,

'So that ye for them are made
Loom and plough and sword and spade,
With or without your own will bent
To their defence and nourishment;

' 'Tis to see your children weak
With their mothers pine and peak
When the winter winds are bleak—
They are dying whilst I speak;

' 'Tis to hunger for such diet
As the rich man in his riot
Casts to the fat dogs that lie
Surfeiting beneath his eye;

' 'Tis to let the Ghost of Gold
Take from Toil a thousandfold
More than e'er its substance could
In the tyrannies of old—

'Paper coin, that forgery
Of the title deeds, which ye
Hold to something from the worth
Of the inheritance of Earth;

' 'Tis to be a slave in soul
And to hold no strong control
Over your own will, but be
All that others make of ye;

'And at length when ye complain
With a murmur weak and vain,
'Tis to see the tyrants' crew
Ride over your wives and you—
Blood is on the grass like dew.

'Then it is to feel revenge
Fiercely thirsting to exchange
Blood for blood, and wrong for wrong—
Do not thus when ye are strong.

'Birds find rest, in narrow nest
When weary of their wingèd quest,
Beasts find fare, in woody lair
When storm and snow are in the air;

'Horses, oxen, have a home
When from daily toil they come;
Household dogs, when the wind roars
Find a home within warm doors;

'Asses, swine, have litter spread
And with fitting food are fed;
All things have a home but one—
Thou, O Englishman, hast none!

'This is slavery—savage men
Or wild beasts within a den
Would endure not as ye do—
But such ills they never knew.

'What art thou, Freedom? O, could slaves
Answer from their living graves
This demand, tyrants would flee
Like a dream's dim imagery.

'Thou art not as imposters say
A Shadow soon to pass away,
A Superstition, and a name
Echoing from the cave of Fame:

'For the labourer thou art bread
And a comely table spread,
From his daily labour come,
In a neat and happy home;

'Thou art clothes and fire and food
For the trampled multitude—
No—in countries that are free
Such starvation cannot be
As in England now we see.

'To the rich thou art a check—
When his foot is on the neck
Of his victim, thou dost make
That he treads upon a snake.

'Thou art Justice—ne'er for gold
May thy righteous laws be sold
As laws are in England—thou
Shieldst alike both high and low.

'Thou art Wisdom—Freemen never
Dream that God will damn forever
All who think those things untrue
Of which Priests make such ado.

'Thou art Peace—never by thee
Would blood and treasure wasted be
As tyrants wasted them, when all
Leagued to quench thy flame in Gaul.

'What if English toil and blood
Was poured forth even as a flood?
It availed, O Liberty,
To dim, but not extinguish thee.

'Thou art Love—the rich have kissed
Thy feet, and like him following Christ
Give their substance to the free
And through the rough world follow thee,

'Or turn their wealth to arms, and make
War for thy belovèd sake
On wealth and war and fraud—whence they
Drew the power which is their prey.

'Science, Poetry and Thought
Are thy lamps; they make the lot
Of the dwellers in a cot
Such, they curse their Maker not.

'Spirit, Patience, Gentleness,
All that can adorn and bless
Art thou . . . let deeds not words express
Thine exceeding loveliness—

'Let a great Assembly be
Of the fearless and the free
On some spot of English ground
Where the plains stretch wide around.

'Let the blue sky overhead,
The green earth on which ye tread,
All that must eternal be
Witness the Solemnity.

'From the corners uttermost
Of the bounds of English coast,
From every hut, village and town
Where those who live and suffer, moan
For others' misery or their own—

'From the workhouse and the prison
Where pale as corpses newly risen
Women, children, young and old
Groan for pain and weep for cold—

'From the haunts of daily life
Where is waged the daily strife
With common wants and common cares
Which sows the human heart with tares—

'Lastly from the palaces
Where the murmur of distress
Echoes, like the distant sound
Of a wind alive around

'Those prison-halls of wealth and fashion
Where some few feel such compassion
For those who groan and toil and wail
As must make their brethren pale,

'Ye who suffer woes untold
Or to feel or to behold
Your lost country bought and sold
With a price of blood and gold—

'Let a vast Assembly be,
And with great solemnity
Declare with measured words that ye
Are, as God has made ye, free—

'Be your strong and simple words
Keen to wound as sharpened swords,
And wide as targes let them be
With their shade to cover ye.

'Let the tyrants pour around
With a quick and startling sound
Like the loosening of a sea
Troops of armed emblazonry.

'Let the charged artillery drive
Till the dead air seems alive
With the clash of clanging wheels
And the tramp of horses' heels.

'Let the fixèd bayonet
Gleam with sharp desire to wet
Its bright point in English blood—
Looking keen, as one for food.

'Let the horsemen's scimitars
Wheel and flash like sphereless stars
Thirsting to eclipse their burning
In a sea of death and mourning.

'Stand ye calm and resolute
Like a forest close and mute
With folded arms and looks which are
Weapons of unvanquished war,

'And let Panic who outspeeds
The career of armed steeds
Pass, a disregarded shade,
Through your phalanx undismayed.

'Let the Laws of your own land,
Good or ill, between ye stand
Hand to hand and foot to foot,
Arbiters of the dispute,

'The old laws of England—they
Whose reverend heads with age are grey,
Children of a wiser day,
And whose solemn voice must be
Thine own echo—Liberty!

'One those who first should violate
Such sacred heralds in their state
Rest the blood that must ensue ...
And it will not rest on you.

'And if then the tyrants dare,
Let them ride among you there,
Slash and stab and maim and hew—
What they like, that let them do.

'With folded arms, and steady eyes,
And little fear, and less surprise,
Look upon them as they slay
Till their rage has died away.

'Then they will return with shame
To the place from which they came,
And the blood thus shed will speak
In hot blushes on their cheek:

'Every Woman in the land
Will point at them as they stand . . .
They will hardly dare to greet
Their acquaintance in the street.

'And the bold, true warriors
Who have hugged Danger in wars
Will turn to those who would be free,
Ashamed of such base company.

'And that slaughter, to the Nation
Shall steam up like inspiration,
Eloquent, oracular;
A volcano heard afar.

'And these words shall then become
Like oppression's thundered doom
Ringing through each heart and brain,
Heard again—again—again—'

'Rise like Lions after slumber
In unvanquishable number—
Shake your chains to earth like dew
Which in sleep had fallen on you—
Ye are many—they are few.'

From PETER BELL THE THIRD
Part the third: HELL

Hell is a city much like London—
    A populous and a smoky city;
There are all sorts of people undone,
And there is little or no fun done;
    Small justice shown, and still less pity.

There is a Castle, and a Canning,
    A Cobbett, and a Castlereagh;
All sorts of caitiff corpses planning
All sorts of cozening for trepanning
    Corpses less corrupt than they.

There is a ***, who has lost
    His wits, or sold them, none knows which;
He walks about a double ghost,
And though as thin as Fraud almost—
    Ever grows more grim and rich.

There is a Chancery Court; a King;
    A manufacturing mob; a set
Of thieves who by themselves are sent
Similar thieves to represent;
    An army; and a public debt—

Which last is a scheme of Paper money,
    And means—being interpreted—
'Bees, keep your wax—give us the honey,
And we will plant while skies are sunny,
    Flowers, which in winter serve instead.'

There is great talk of Revolution—
    And a great chance of Despotism—
German soldiers—camps—confusion—
Tumults—lotteries—rage—delusion—
    Gin—suicide—and methodism.

Taxes too, on wine and bread,
    And meat, and beer, and tea, and cheese,
From which those patriots pure are fed,
Who gorge before they reel to bed
    The tenfold essence of all these.

There are mincing women, mewing
    (Like cats, who *amant miserè*,)
Of their own virtue, and pursuing
Their gentler sisters to that ruin,
    Without which—what were chastity?

Lawyers—judges—old hobnobbers
　　Are there—bailiffs—chancellors—
Bishops—great and little robbers—
Rhymesters—pamphleteers—stock-jobbers—
　　Men of glory in the wars,—

Things whose trade is, over ladies
　　To lean, and flirt, and stare, and simper,
Till all that is divine in woman
Grows cruel, courteous, smooth, inhuman,
　　Crucified 'twixt a smile and whimper.

Thrusting, toiling, wailing, moiling,
　　Frowning, preaching—such a riot!
Each with never-ceasing labour,
Whilst he thinks he cheats his neighbour,
　　Cheating his own heart of quiet.

And all these meet at levees;—
　　Dinners convivial and political;—
Suppers of epic poets;—teas,
Where small talk dies in agonies;—
　　Breakfasts professional and critical;—

Lunches and snacks so aldermanic
    That one would furnish forth ten dinners,
Where reigns a Cretan-tonguèd panic
Lest news Russ, Dutch, or Alemannic
    Should make some losers, and some winners;-

At conversazioni—balls—
    Conventicles—and drawing-rooms—
Courts of law—committees—calls
Of a morning—clubs—book-stalls—
    Churches—masquerades—and tombs.

And this is Hell—and in this smother
    All are damnable and damned;
Each one damning, damns the other;
They are damned by one another,
    By none other are they damned.

'Tis a lie to say, 'God damns!'
    Where was Heaven's Attorney General
When they first gave out such flams?
Let there be an end of shams,
    They are mines of poisonous mineral.

Statesmen damn themselves to be
   Cursed; and lawyers damn their souls
To the auction of a fee;
Churchmen damn themselves to see
   God's sweet love in burning coals.

The rich are damned, beyond all cure,
   To taunt, and starve, and trample on
The weak and wretched; and the poor
Damn their broken hearts to endure
   Stripe on stripe, with groan on groan.

Sometimes the poor are damned indeed
   To take,—not means for being blest,—
But Cobbett's snuff, revenge; that weed
From which the worms that it doth feed
   Squeeze less than they before possessed.

And some few, like we know who,
   Damned—but God alone knows why—
To believe their minds are given
To make this ugly Hell a Heaven;
   In which faith they live and die.

Thus, as in a town plague-stricken,
    Each man be he sound or no
Must indifferently sicken;
As when day begins to thicken,
    None knows a pigeon from a crow,—

So good and bad, sane and mad,
    The oppressor and the oppressed;
Those who weep to see what others
Smile to inflict upon their brothers;
    Lovers, haters, worst and best;

All are damned—they breathe an air
    Thick, infected, joy-dispelling:
Each pursues what seems most fair,
Mining like moles through mind, and there
Scoop palace-caverns vast, where Care
    In thronèd state is ever dwelling.

Part the fourth: SIN

Lo, Peter in Hell's Grosvenor-square,
  A footman in the devil's service!
And the misjudging world would swear
That every man in service there
  To virtue would prefer vice.

But Peter, though now damned, was not
  What Peter was before damnation.
Men oftentimes prepare a lot
Which, ere it finds them, is not what
  Suits with their genuine station.

All things that Peter saw and felt
  Had a peculiar aspect to him;
And when they came within the belt
Of his own nature, seemed to melt,
  Like cloud to cloud, into him.

And so, the outward world uniting
  To that within him, he became
Considerably uninviting
To those, who meditation slighting,
  Were moulded in a different frame.

And he scorned them, and they scorned him;
　　And he scorned all they did; and they
Did all that men of their own trim
Are wont to do to please their whim,—
　　Drinking, lying, swearing, play.

Such were his fellow-servants; thus
　　His virtue, like our own, was built
Too much on that indignant fuss
Hypocrite Pride stirs up in us
　　To bully one another's guilt.

He had a mind which was somehow
　　At once circumference and centre
Of all he might or feel or know;
Nothing went ever out, although
　　Something did ever enter.

He had as much imagination
　　As a pint-pot:—he never could
Fancy another situation,
From which to dart his contemplation,
　　Than that wherein he stood.

Yet his was individual mind,
    And new created all he saw
In a new manner, and refined
Those new creations, and combined
    Them, by a master-spirit's law.

Thus—though unimaginative—
    An apprehension clear, intense,
Of his mind's work, had made alive
The things it wrought on; I believe,
    Wakening a sort of thought in sense.

But from the first 'twas Peter's drift
    To be a kind of moral eunuch,
He touched the hem of nature's shift,
Felt faint—and never dared uplift
    The closest, all-concealing tunic.

She laughed the while, with an arch smile,
    And kissed him with a sister's kiss,
And said—'My best Diogenes,
I love you well—but, if you please,
    Tempt not again my deepest bliss.

'"Tis you are cold—for I, not coy,
    Yield love for love, frank, warm and true;
And Burns, a Scottish peasant boy—
His errors prove it—knew my joy
    More, learned friend, than you.

'*Bocca baciata non perde ventura*
    Anzi rinnuova come fa la luna:—
So thought Boccaccio, whose sweet words might cure a
Male prude, like you, from what you now endure, a
    Low-tide in soul, like a stagnant laguna.'

Then Peter rubbed his eyes severe,
    And smoothed his spacious forehead down
With his broad palm:—'twixt love and fear,
He looked, as he no doubt felt, queer;
    And in his dream sate down.

The Devil was no uncommon creature;
    A leaden-witted thief—just huddled
Out of the dross and scum of nature;
A toad-like lump of limb and feature,
    With mind, and heart, and fancy muddled.

He was that heavy, dull, cold thing
    The Spirit of Evil well may be:
A drone too base to have a sting;
Who gluts, and grimes his lazy wing,
    And calls lust, luxury.

Now he was quite the kind of wight
    Round whom collect, at a fixed era,
Venison, turtle, hock and claret,—
Good cheer—and those who come to share it—
    And best East Indian madeira!

It was his fancy to invite
    Men of science, wit and learning,
Who came to lend each other light:—
He proudly thought that his gold's might
    Had set those spirits burning.

And men of learning, science, wit,
    Considered him as you and I
Think of some rotten tree, and sit
Lounging and dining under it,
    Exposed to the wide sky.

And all the while, with loose fat smile
    The willing wretch sat winking there,
Believing 'twas his power that made
That jovial scene—and that all paid
    Homage to his unnoticed chair.

Though to be sure this place was Hell;
    He was the Devil—and all they—
What though the claret circled well,
And wit, like ocean, rose and fell?—
    Were damned eternally.

Part the fifth: GRACE

Among the guests who often stayed
   Till the Devil's petits-soupers,
A man there came, fair as a maid,
And Peter noted what he said,
   Standing behind his master's chair.

He was a mighty poet—and
   A subtle-souled psychologist;
All things he seemed to understand,
Of old or new—of sea or land—
   But his own mind—which was a mist.

This was a man who might have turned
   Hell into Heaven—and so in gladness
A Heaven unto himself have earned;
But he in shadows undiscerned
   Trusted,—and damned himself to madness.

He spoke of Poetry, and how
   'Divine it was—a light—a love—
A spirit which like wind doth blow
As it listeth, to and fro;
   A dew rained down from God above;

'A Power which comes and goes like dream,
    And which none can ever trace—
Heaven's light on Earth—Truth's brightest beam.'
And when he ceased there lay the gleam
    Of those words upon his face.

Now Peter when he heard such talk
    Would, heedless of a broken pate
Stand like a man asleep, or baulk
Some wishing guest of knife or fork,
    Or drop and break his master's plate.

At night he oft would start and wake
    Like a lover, and began
In a wild measure songs to make
On moor, and glen, and rocky lake,
    And on the heart of man;—

And on the universal sky;—
    And the wide earth's bosom green;—
And the sweet, strange mystery
Of what beyond these things may lie,
    And yet remain unseen.

For in his thought he visited
    The spots in which, ere dead and damned,
He his wayward life had led;
Yet knew not whence the thoughts were fed,
    Which thus his fancy crammed.

And these obscure remembrances
    Stirred such harmony in Peter,
That, whensoever he should please,
He could speak of rocks and trees
    In poetic metre.

For though it was without a sense
    Of memory, yet he remembered well
Many a ditch and quick-set fence;
Of lakes he had intelligence,
    He knew something of heath, and fell.

He had also dim recollections
    Of pedlars tramping on their rounds;
Milk-pans and pails; and odd collections
Of saws and proverbs; and reflections
    Old parsons make in burying-grounds.

But Peter's verse was clear, and came
    Announcing from the frozen hearth
Of a cold age, that none might tame
The soul of that diviner flame
    It augured to the Earth:

Like gentle rains, on the dry plains,
    Making that green which late was grey,
Or like the sudden moon, that stains
Some gloomy chamber's window panes
    With a broad light like day.

For language was in Peter's hand,
    Like clay, while he was yet a potter;
And he made songs for all the land,
Sweet both to feel and understand,
    As pipkins late to mountain cotter.

And Mr.—, the bookseller,
    Gave twenty pounds for some;—then scorning
A footman's yellow coat to wear,
Peter, too proud of heart, I fear,
    Instantly gave the Devil warning.

Whereat the Devil took offence,
　　And swore in his soul a great oath then,
'That for his damned impertinence,
He'd bring him to a proper sense
　　Of what was due to gentlemen!' —

LINES WRITTEN ON HEARING THE NEWS OF THE DEATH OF NAPOLEON

What! alive and so bold, O Earth?
  Art thou not overbold?
  What! leapest thou forth as of old
In the light of thy morning mirth,
The last of the flock of the starry fold?
Ha! leapest thou forth as of old?
Are not the limbs still when the ghost is fled,
And canst thou move, Napoleon being dead?

How! is not thy quick heart cold?
  What spark is alive on thy hearth?
How! is not *his* death-knell knolled?
  And livest *thou* still, Mother Earth?
Thou wert warming thy fingers old
O'er the embers covered and cold
Of that most fiery spirit, when it fled—
What, Mother, do you laugh now he is dead?

'Who has known me of old,' replied Earth,
  'Or who has my story told?
  It is thou who art overbold.'
And the lightning of scorn laughed forth
As she sung, 'To my bosom I fold
All my sons when their knell is knolled,
And so with living motion all are fed,
And the quick spring like weeds out of the dead.

'Still alive and still bold,' shouted Earth,
  'I grow bolder and still more bold.
  The dead fill me ten thousandfold
Fuller of speed, and splendour, and mirth.
I was cloudy, and sullen, and cold,
Like a frozen chaos uprolled,
Till by the spirit of the mighty dead
My heart grew warm. I feed on whom I fed.

'Aye, alive and still bold,' muttered Earth.
  'Napoleon's fierce spirit rolled,
  In terror and blood and gold,
A torrent of ruin to death from his birth.
Leave the millions who follow to mould
The metal before it be cold;
And weave into his shame, which like the dead
Shrouds me, the hopes that from his glory fled.'

HYMN TO INTELLECTUAL BEAUTY

1. The awful shadow of some unseen Power
    Floats though unseen amongst us,—visiting
    This various world with as inconstant wing
As summer winds that creep from flower to flower.—
Like moonbeams that behind some piny mountain
        It visits with inconstant glance   [shower,
        Each human heart and countenance;
Like hues and harmonies of evening,—
        Like clouds in starlight widely spread,—
        Like memory of music fled,—
        Like aught that for its grace may be
Dear, and yet dearer for its mystery.

2. Spirit of BEAUTY, that doth consecrate
        With thine own hues all thou dost shine upon
        Of human thought or form,—where art thou gone?
Why dost thou pass away and leave our state,
This dim vast vale of tears, vacant and desolate?
        Ask why the sunlight not forever
        Weaves rainbows o'er yon mountain river,
Why aught should fail and fade that once is shown,
        Why fear and dream and death and birth
        Cast on the daylight of this earth
        Such gloom,—why man has such a scope
For love and hate, despondency and hope?

3. No voice from some sublimer world hath ever
       To sage or poet these responses given—
       Therefore the name of God and ghosts and Heaven,
   Remain the records of their vain endeavour,
   Frail spells—whose uttered charm might not avail
           From all we hear and all we see,   [to sever
           Doubt, chance, and mutability.
   Thy light alone—like mist o'er mountains driven,
           Or music by the night wind sent
           Through strings of some still instrument,
           Or moonlight on a midnight stream,
   Gives grace and truth to life's unquiet dream.

4. Love, Hope, and Self-esteem, like clouds depart
       And come, for some uncertain moments lent.
       Man were immortal, and omnipotent,
   Didst thou, unknown and awful as thou art,
   Keep with thy glorious train firm state within his
           Thou messenger of sympathies,   [heart.
           That wax and wane in lovers' eyes—
   Thou—that to human thought art nourishment,
           Like darkness to a dying flame!
           Depart not as thy shadow came,
           Depart not—lest the grave should be,
   Like life and fear, a dark reality.

5. While yet a boy I sought for ghosts, and sped
        Through many a listening chamber, cave and ruin,
        And starlight wood, with fearful steps pursuing
    Hopes of high talk with the departed dead.
    I called on poisonous names with which our youth is
            I was not heard—I saw them not—   ⌈fed,
            When musing deeply on the lot
        Of life, at that sweet time when winds are wooing
            All vital things that wake to bring
            News of buds and blossoming,—
            Sudden, thy shadow fell on me;
    I shrieked, and clasped my hands in ecstasy!

6. I vowed that I would dedicate my powers
        To thee and thine—have I not kept the vow?
        With beating heart and streaming eyes, even now
    I call the phantoms of a thousand hours
    Each from his voiceless grave: they have in visioned
            Of studious zeal or love's delight   ⌈bowers
            Outwatched with me the envious night—
        They know that never joy illumed my brow
            Unlinked with hope that thou wouldst free
            This world from its dark slavery,
            That thou—O awful LOVELINESS,
    Wouldst give whate'er these words cannot express.

7. The day becomes more solemn and serene
       When noon is past—there is a harmony
       In autumn, and a lustre in its sky,
    Which through the summer is not heard or seen,
    As if it could not be, as if it had not been!
           Thus let thy power, which like the truth
           Of nature on my passive youth
    Descended, to my onward life supply
           Its calm—to one who worships thee,
           And every form containing thee,
           Whom, SPIRIT fair, thy spells did bind
    To fear himself, and love all human kind.

MONT BLANC
Lines Written in the Vale of Chamouni

1. The everlasting universe of things
   Flows through the mind, and rolls its rapid waves,
   Now dark—now glittering—now reflecting gloom—
   Now lending splendour, where from secret springs
   The source of human thought its tribute brings
   Of waters,—with a sound but half its own,
   Such as a feeble brook will oft assume
   In the wild woods, among the mountains lone,
   Where waterfalls around it leap forever,
   Where woods and winds contend, and a vast river
   Over its rocks ceaselessly bursts and raves.

2. Thus thou, Ravine of Arve—dark, deep Ravine—
   Thou many-coloured, many-voicèd vale,
   Over whose pines, and crags, and caverns sail
   Fast cloud-shadows and sunbeams: awful scene,
   Where Power in likeness of the Arve comes down
   From the ice gulfs that gird his secret throne,
   Bursting through these dark mountains like the flame
   Of lightning through the tempest;—thou dost lie,
   Thy giant brood of pines around thee clinging,
   Children of elder time, in whose devotion
   The chainless winds still come and ever came
   To drink their odours, and their mighty swinging

To hear—an old and solemn harmony;
Thine earthly rainbows stretched across the sweep
Of the aethereal waterfall, whose veil
Robes some unsculptured image; the strange sleep
Which when the voices of the desert fail
Wraps all in its own deep eternity;—
Thy caverns echoing to the Arve's commotion,
A loud, lone sound no other sound can tame;
Thou art pervaded with that ceaseless motion,
Thou art the path of that unresting sound—
Dizzy Ravine!—and when I gaze on thee
I seem as in a trance sublime and strange
To muse on my own separate phantasy,
My own, my human mind, which passively
Now renders and receives fast influencings,
Holding an unremitting interchange
With the clear universe of things around;
One legion of wild thoughts, whose wandering wings
Now float above thy darkness, and now rest
Where that or thou art no unbidden guest,
In the still cave of the witch Poesy,
Seeking among the shadows that pass by,
Ghosts of all things that are, some shade of thee,
Some phantom, some faint image; till the breast
From which they fled recalls them, thou art there!

3. Some say that gleams of a remoter world
   Visit the soul in sleep,—that death is slumber,
   And that its shapes the busy thoughts outnumber
   Of those who wake and live.—I look on high:—
   Has some unknown omnipotence unfurled
   The veil of life and death? or do I lie
   In dream, and does the mightier world of sleep
   Spread far around and inaccessibly
   Its circles? For the very spirit fails,
   Driven like a homeless cloud from steep to steep
   That vanishes among the viewless gales!
   Far, far above, piercing the infinite sky,
   Mont Blanc appears,—still, snowy, and serene;
   Its subject mountains their unearthly forms
   Pile round it, ice and rock; broad vales between
   Of frozen floods, unfathomable deeps,
   Blue as the overhanging heaven, that spread
   And wind among the accumulated steeps:—
   A desert peopled by the storms alone,
   Save when the eagle brings some hunter's bone,
   And the wolf tracks her there—how hideously
   Its shapes are heaped around! rude, bare, and high,
   Ghastly, and scarred, and riven.—Is this the scene
   Where the old Earthquake-dæmon taught her young
   Ruin? Were these their toys? or did a sea
   Of fire envelop once this silent snow?
   None can reply—all seems eternal now.

The wilderness has a mysterious tongue
Which teaches awful doubt, or faith so mild,
So solemn, so serene, that man may be
But for such faith with nature reconciled;
Thou hast a voice, great Mountain, to repeal
Large codes of fraud and woe; not understood
By all, but which the wise, and great, and good
Interpret, or make felt, or deeply feel.

The fields, the lakes, the forests, and the streams,
Ocean, and all the living things that dwell
Within the dædal earth; lightning, and rain,
Earthquake, and fiery flood, and hurricane,
The torpor of the year when feeble dreams
Visit the hidden buds, or dreamless sleep
Holds every future leaf and flower;—the bound
With which from that detested trance they leap;
The works and ways of man, their death and birth,
And that of him and all that his may be;
All things that move and breathe with toil and sound
Are born and die; revolve, subside and swell.
Power dwells apart in its tranquillity
Remote, serene, and inaccessible:
And *this*, the naked countenance of earth,
On which I gaze, even these primæval mountains
Teach the adverting mind. The glaciers creep
Like snakes that watch their prey, from their far
[fountains,

Slow rolling on; there, many a precipice,
Frost and the Sun in scorn of mortal power
Have piled: dome, pyramid, and pinnacle,
A city of death, distinct with many a tower
And wall impregnable of beaming ice.
Yet not a city, but a flood of ruin
Is there, that from the boundaries of the sky
Rolls its perpetual stream; vast pines are strewing
Its destined path, or in the mangled soil
Branchless and shattered stand; the rocks, drawn down
From yon remotest waste, have overthrown
The limits of the dead and living world,
Never to be reclaimed. The dwelling-place
Of insects, beasts, and birds becomes its spoil;
Their food and their retreat forever gone,
So much of life and joy is lost. The race
Of man flies far in dread; his work and dwelling
Vanish, like smoke before the tempest's stream,
And their place is not known. Below, vast caves
Shine in the rushing torrents' restless gleam,
Which from those secret chasms in tumult welling
Meet in the vale, and one majestic River,
The breath and blood of distant lands, forever
Rolls its loud waters to the ocean waves,
Breathes its swift vapours to the circling air.

5. Mont Blanc yet gleams on high:—the power is there,
   The still and solemn power of many sights,
   And many sounds, and much of life and death.
   In the calm darkness of the moonless nights,
   In the lone glare of day, the snows descend
   Upon that Mountain; none beholds them there,
   Nor when the flakes burn in the sinking sun,
   Or the star-beams dart through them.—Winds
                                                      ⌈contend

   Silently there, and heap the snow with breath
   Rapid and strong, but silently! Its home
   The voiceless lightning in these solitudes
   Keeps innocently, and like vapour broods
   Over the snow. The secret strength of things
   Which governs thought, and to the infinite dome
   Of heaven is as a law, inhabits thee!
   And what were thou, and earth, and stars, and sea,
   If to the human mind's imaginings
   Silence and solitude were vacancy?

DRAMATIC
AND
NARRATIVE
POEMS

From ALASTOR, *or*
THE SPIRIT OF SOLITUDE

There was a Poet whose untimely tomb
No human hands with pious reverence reared,
But the charmed eddies of autumnal winds
Built o'er his mouldering bones a pyramid
Of mouldering leaves in the waste wilderness:—
A lovely youth,—no mourning maiden decked
With weeping flowers, or votive cypress wreath,
The lone couch of his everlasting sleep:—
Gentle, and brave, and generous,—no lorn bard
Breathed o'er his dark fate one melodious sigh:
He lived, he died, he sung, in solitude.
Strangers have wept to hear his passionate notes,
And virgins, as unknown he passed, have pined
And wasted for fond love of his wild eyes.
The fire of those soft orbs has ceased to burn,
And Silence, too enamoured of that voice,
Locks its mute music in her rugged cell.

By solemn vision, and bright silver dream,
His infancy was nurtured. Every sight
And sound from the vast earth and ambient air,
Sent to his heart its choicest impulses.
The fountains of divine philosophy
Fled not his thirsting lips, and all of great,

Or good, or lovely, which the sacred past
In truth or fable consecrates, he felt
And knew. When early youth had passed, he left
His cold fireside and alienated home
To seek strange truths in undiscovered lands.
Many a wide waste and tangled wilderness
Has lured his fearless steps; and he has bought
With his sweet voice and eyes, from savage men,
His rest and food. Nature's most secret steps
He like her shadow has pursued, where'er
The red volcano overcanopies
Its fields of snow and pinnacles of ice
With burning smoke, or where bitumen lakes
On black bare pointed islets ever beat
With sluggish surge, or where the secret caves
Rugged and dark, winding among the springs
Of fire and poison, inaccessible
To avarice or pride, their starry domes
Of diamond and of gold expand above
Numberless and immeasurable halls,
Frequent with crystal column, and clear shrines
Of pearl, and thrones radiant with chrysolite.
Nor had that scene of ampler majesty
Than gems or gold, the varying roof of heaven
And the green earth lost in his heart its claims
To love and wonder; he would linger long
In lonesome vales, making the wild his home,

Until the doves and squirrels would partake
From his innocuous hand his bloodless food,
Lured by the gentle meaning of his looks,
And the wild antelope, that starts whene'er
The dry leaf rustles in the brake, suspend
Her timid steps to gaze upon a form
More graceful than her own.

LINES WRITTEN AMONG
THE EUGANEAN HILLS

Many a green isle needs must be
In the deep wide sea of Misery,
Or the mariner, worn and wan,
Never thus could voyage on—
Day and night, and night and day,
Drifting on his dreary way,
With the solid darkness black
Closing round his vessel's track;
Whilst above the sunless sky,
Big with clouds, hangs heavily,
And behind the tempest fleet
Hurries on with lightning feet,
Riving sail, and cord, and plank,
Till the ship has almost drank
Death from the o'er-brimming deep;
And sinks down, down, like that sleep
When the dreamer seems to be
Weltering through eternity;
And the dim low line before
Of a dark and distant shore
Still recedes, as ever still
Longing with divided will,
But no power to seek or shun,
He is ever drifted on

O'er the unreposing wave
To the haven of the grave.
What, if there no friends will greet;
What, if there no heart will meet
His with love's impatient beat;
Wander wheresoe'er he may,
Can he dream before that day
To find refuge from distress
In friendship's smile, in love's caress?
Then 'twill wreak him little woe
Whether such there be or no:
Senseless is the breast, and cold,
Which relenting love would fold;
Bloodless are the veins and chill
Which the pulse of pain did fill;
Every little living nerve
That from bitter words did swerve
Round the tortured lips and brow,
Are like sapless leaflets now
Frozen upon December's bough.

On the beach of a northern sea
Which tempests shake eternally,
As once the wretch there lay to sleep,
Lies a solitary heap,
One white skull and seven dry bones,
On the margin of the stones,

Where a few gray rushes stand,
Boundaries of the sea and land:
Nor is heard one voice of wail
But the sea-mews, as they sail
O'er the billows of the gale;
Or the whirlwind up and down
Howling, like a slaughtered town,
When a king in glory rides
Through the pomp of fratricides:
Those unburied bones around
There is many a mournful sound;
There is no lament for him,
Like a sunless vapour, dim,
Who once clothed with life and thought
What now moves nor murmurs not.

Ay, many flowering islands lie
In the waters of wide Agony:
To such a one this morn was led,
My bark by soft winds piloted:
'Mid the mountains Euganean
I stood listening to the paean
With which the legioned rooks did hail
The sun's uprise majestical;
Gathering round with wings all hoar,
Through the dewy mist they soar
Like gray shades, till the eastern heaven

Bursts, and then, as clouds of even,
Flecked with fire and azure, lie
In the unfathomable sky,
So their plumes of purple grain,
Starred with drops of golden rain,
Gleam above the sunlight woods,
As in silent multitudes
On the morning's fitful gale
Through the broken mist they sail,
And the vapours cloven and gleaming
Follow, down the dark steep streaming,
Till all is bright, and clear, and still,
Round the solitary hill.

Beneath is spread like a green sea
The waveless plain of Lombardy,
Bounded by the vaporous air,
Islanded by cities fair;
Underneath Day's azure eyes
Ocean's nursling, Venice lies,
A peopled labyrinth of walls,
Amphitrite's destined halls,
Which her hoary sire now paves
With his blue and beaming waves.
Lo! the sun upsprings behind,
Broad, red, radiant, half-reclined
On the level quivering line

Of the waters crystalline;
And before that chasm of light,
As within a furnace bright,
Column, tower, and dome, and spire,
Shine like obelisks of fire,
Pointing with inconstant motion
From the altar of dark ocean
To the sapphire-tinted skies;
As the flames of sacrifice
From the marble shrines did rise,
As to pierce the dome of gold
Where Apollo spoke of old.

Sun-girt City, thou hast been
Ocean's child, and then his queen;
Now is come a darker day,
And thou soon must be his prey,
If the power that raised thee here
Hallow so thy watery bier.
A less drear ruin then than now,
With thy conquest-branded brow
Stooping to the slave of slaves
From thy throne, among the waves
Wilt thou be, when the sea-mew
Flies, as once before it flew,
O'er thine isles depopulate,
And all is in its ancient state,

Save where many a palace gate
With green sea-flowers overgrown
Like a rock of Ocean's own,
Topples o'er the abandoned sea
As the tides change sullenly.
The fisher on his watery way,
Wandering at the close of day,
Will spread his sail and seize his oar
Till he pass the gloomy shore,
Lest thy dead should, from their sleep
Bursting o'er the starlight deep,
Lead a rapid masque of death
O'er the waters of his path.

Those who alone thy towers behold
Quivering through aëreal gold,
As I now behold them here,
Would imagine not they were
Sepulchres, where human forms,
Like pollution-nourished worms,
To the corpse of greatness cling,
Murdered, and now mouldering:
But if Freedom should awake
In her omnipotence, and shake
From the Celtic Anarch's hold
All the keys of dungeons cold,
Where a hundred cities lie

Chained like thee, ingloriously,
Thou and all thy sister band
Might adorn this sunny land,
Twining memories of old time
With new virtues more sublime;
If not, perish thou and they!—
Clouds which stain truth's rising day
By her sun consumed away—
Earth can spare ye: while like flowers,
In the waste of years and hours,
From your dust new nations spring
With more kindly blossoming.

Perish—let there only be
Floating o'er thy hearthless sea
As the garment of thy sky
Clothes the world immortally,
One remembrance, more sublime
Than the tattered pall of time,
Which scarce hides thy visage wan;—
That a tempest-cleaving Swan
Of the songs of Albion,
Driven from his ancestral streams
By the might of evil dreams,
Found a nest in thee; and Ocean
Welcomed him with such emotion
That its joy grew his, and sprung

From his lips like music flung
O'er a mighty thunder-fit,
Chastening terror:—what though yet
Poesy's unfailing River,
Which through Albion winds forever
Lashing with melodious wave
Many a sacred Poet's grave,
Mourn its latest nursling fled?
What though thou with all thy dead
Scarce can for this fame repay
Aught thine own? oh, rather say
Though thy sins and slaveries foul
Overcloud a sunlike soul?
As the ghost of Homer clings
Round Scamander's wasting springs;
As divinest Shakespeare's might
Fills Avon and the world with light
Like omniscient power which he
Imaged 'mid mortality;
As the love from Petrarch's urn,
Yet amid yon hills doth burn,
A quenchless lamp by which the heart
Sees things unearthly;—so thou art,
Mighty spirit—so shall be
The City that did refuge thee.

Lo, the sun floats up the sky
Like thought-wingèd Liberty,
Till the universal light
Seems to level plain and height;
From the sea a mist has spread,
And the beams of morn lie dead
On the towers of Venice now,
Like its glory long ago.
By the skirts of that gray cloud
Many-domèd Padua proud
Stands, a peopled solitude,
'Mid the harvest-shining plain,
Where the peasant heaps his grain
In the garner of his foe,
And the milk-white oxen slow
With the purple vintage strain,
Heaped upon the creaking wain,
That the brutal Celt may swill
Drunken sleep with savage will;
And the sickle to the sword
Lies unchanged, though many a lord,
Like a weed whose shade is poison,
Overgrows this region's foison,
Sheaves of whom are ripe to come
To destruction's harvest-home:
Men must reap the things they sow,
Force from force must ever flow,

Or worse; but 'tis a bitter woe
That love or reason cannot change
The despot's rage, the slave's revenge.

Padua, thou within whose walls
Those mute guests at festivals,
Son and Mother, Death and Sin,
Played at dice for Ezzelin,
Till Death cried, 'I win, I win!'
And Sin cursed to lose the wager,
But Death promised, to assuage her,
That he would petition for
Her to be made Vice-Emperor,
When the destined years were o'er,
Over all between the Po
And the eastern Alpine snow,
Under the mighty Austrian.
Sin smiled so as Sin only can,
And since that time, ay, long before,
Both have ruled from shore to shore,—
That incestuous pair, who follow
Tyrants as the sun the swallow,
As Repentance follows Crime,
And as changes follow Time.

In thine halls the lamp of learning,
Padua, now no more is burning;

Like a meteor, whose wild way
Is lost over the grave of day,
It gleams betrayed and to betray:
Once remotest nations came
To adore that sacred flame,
When it lit not many a hearth
On this cold and gloomy earth:
Now new fires from antique light
Spring beneath the wide world's might;
But their spark lies dead in thee,
Trampled out by Tyranny.
As the Norway woodman quells,
In the depth of piny dells,
One light flame among the brakes,
While the boundless forest shakes,
And its mighty trunks are torn
By the fire thus lowly born:
The spark beneath his feet is dead,
He starts to see the flames it fed
Howling through the darkened sky
With a myriad tongues victoriously,
And sinks down in fear: so thou,
O Tyranny, beholdest now
Light around thee, and thou hearest
The loud flames ascend, and fearest:
Grovel on the earth; ay, hide
In the dust thy purple pride!

Noon descends around me now:
'Tis the noon of autumn's glow,
When a soft and purple mist
Like a vaporous amethyst,
Or an air-dissolvèd star
Mingling light and fragrance, far
From the curved horizon's bound
To the point of Heaven's profound,
Fills the overflowing sky;
And the plains that silent lie
Underneath, the leaves unsodden
Where the infant Frost has trodden
With his morning-wingèd feet,
Whose bright print is gleaming yet;
And the red and golden vines,
Piercing with their trellised lines
The rough, dark-skirted wilderness;
The dun and bladed grass no less,
Pointing from this hoary tower
In the windless air; the flower
Glimmering at my feet; the line
Of the olive-sandalled Apennine
In the south dimly islanded;
And the Alps, whose snows are spread
High between the clouds and sun;
And of living things each one;
And my spirit which so long

Darkened this swift stream of song,—
Interpenetrated lie
By the glory of the sky:
Be it love, light, harmony,
Odour, or the soul of all
Which from Heaven like dew doth fall,
Or the mind which feeds this verse
Peopling the lone universe.

Noon descends, and after noon
Autumn's evening meets me soon,
Leading the infantine moon,
And that one star, which to her
Almost seems to minister
Half the crimson light she brings
From the sunset's radiant springs:
And the soft dreams of the morn
(Which like wingèd winds had borne
To that silent isle, which lies
Mid remembered agonies,
The frail bark of this lone being)
Pass, to other sufferers fleeing,
And its ancient pilot, Pain,
Sits beside the helm again.

Other flowering isles must be
In the sea of Life and Agony:

Other spirits float and flee
O'er that gulf: even now, perhaps,
On some rock the wild wave wraps,
With folded wings they waiting sit
For my bark, to pilot it
To some calm and blooming cove,
Where for me, and those I love,
May a windless bower be built,
Far from passion, pain, and guilt,
In a dell mid lawny hills,
Which the wild sea-murmur fills,
And soft sunshine, and the sound
Of old forests echoing round,
And the light and smell divine
Of all flowers that breathe and shine:
We may live so happy there,
That the Spirits of the Air,
Envying us, may even entice
To our healing Paradise
The polluting multitude;
But their rage would be subdued
By that clime divine and calm,
And the winds whose wings rain balm
On the uplifted soul, and leaves
Under which the bright sea heaves;
While each breathless interval
In their whisperings musical

The inspired soul supplies
With its own deep melodies,
And the love which heals all strife
Circling, like the breath of life,
All things in that sweet abode
With its own mild brotherhood:
They, not it, would change; and soon
Every sprite beneath the moon
Would repent its envy vain,
And the earth grow young again.

ADONAIS

I weep for Adonais—he is dead!
O, weep for Adonais! though our tears
Thaw not the frost which binds so dear a head!
And thou, sad Hour, selected from all years
To mourn our loss, rouse thy obscure compeers,
And teach them thine own sorrow, say: with me
Died Adonais; till the Future dares
Forget the Past, his fate and fame shall be
An echo and a light unto eternity!

Where wert thou, mighty Mother, when he lay,
When thy Son lay, pierced by the shaft which flies
In darkness? where was lorn Urania
When Adonais died? With veilèd eyes,
Mid listening Echoes, in her Paradise
She sate, while one, with soft enamoured breath,
Rekindled all the fading melodies
With which, like flowers that mock the corse beneath,
He had adorned and hid the coming bulk of death.

3. O, weep for Adonais—he is dead!
   Wake, melancholy Mother, wake and weep!
   Yet wherefore? Quench within their burning bed
   Thy fiery tears, and let thy loud heart keep
   Like his, a mute and uncomplaining sleep;
   For he is gone, where all things wise and fair
   Descend;—oh, dream not that the amorous Deep
   Will yet restore him to the vital air;
   Death feeds on his mute voice, and laughs at our despair.

4. Most musical of mourners, weep again!
   Lament anew, Urania!—He died,
   Who was the Sire of an immortal strain,
   Blind, old, and lonely, when his country's pride
   The priest, the slave, and the liberticide
   Trampled and mocked with many a loathèd rite
   Of lust and blood; he went, unterrified,
   Into the gulf of death; but his clear Sprite
   Yet reigns o'er earth; the third among the sons of light.

5. Most musical of mourners, weep anew!
   Not all to that bright station dared to climb;
   And happier they their happiness who knew,
   Whose tapers yet burn through that night of time
   In which suns perished; others more sublime,
   Struck by the envious wrath of man or God,
   Have sunk, extinct in their refulgent prime;
   And some yet live, treading the thorny road
   Which leads, through toil and hate, to Fame's serene
   [abode.
6. But now, thy youngest, dearest one, has perished—
   The nursling of thy widowhood, who grew,
   Like a pale flower by some sad maiden cherished,
   And fed with true love tears, instead of dew;
   Most musical of mourners, weep anew!
   Thy extreme hope, the loveliest and the last,
   The bloom, whose petals nipped before they blew
   Died on the promise of the fruit, is waste;
   The broken lily lies—the storm is overpast.

7. To that high Capital, where kingly Death
   Keeps his pale court in beauty and decay,
   He came; and bought, with price of purest breath,
   A grave among the eternal.—Come away!
   Haste, while the vault of blue Italian day
   Is yet his fitting charnel-roof! while still
   He lies, as if in dewy sleep he lay;
   Awake him not! surely he takes his fill
   Of deep and liquid rest, forgetful of all ill.

8. He will awake no more, oh, never more!—
   Within the twilight chamber spreads apace
   The shadow of white Death, and at the door
   Invisible Corruption waits to trace
   His extreme way to her dim dwelling-place;
   The eternal Hunger sits, but pity and awe
   Soothe her pale rage, nor dares she to deface
   So fair a prey, till darkness, and the law
   Of change, shall o'er his sleep the mortal curtain draw.

9. O, weep for Adonais!—The quick Dreams,
    The passion-wingèd Ministers of thought,
    Who were his flocks, whom near the living streams
    Of his young spirit he fed, and whom he taught
    The love which was its music, wander not,—
    Wander no more, from kindling brain to brain,
    But droop there, whence they sprung; and mourn their
                                                    ⌜lot
    Round the cold heart, where, after their sweet pain,
    They ne'er will gather strength, or find a home again.

10. And one with trembling hands clasps his cold head,
    And fans him with her moonlight wings, and cries,
    'Our love, our hope, our sorrow, is not dead;
    See, on the silken fringe of his faint eyes,
    Like dew upon a sleeping flower, there lies
    A tear some Dream has loosened from his brain.'
    Lost Angel of a ruined Paradise!
    She knew not 'twas her own; as with no stain
    She faded, like a cloud which had outwept its rain.

11. One from a lucid urn of starry dew
    Washed his light limbs as if embalming them;
    Another clipped her profuse locks, and threw
    The wreath upon him, like an anadem,
    Which frozen tears instead of pearls begem;
    Another in her wilful grief would break
    Her bow and wingèd reeds, as if to stem
    A greater loss with one which was more weak;
    And dull the barbèd fire against his frozen cheek.

12. Another Splendour on his mouth alit,
    That mouth, whence it was wont to draw the breath
    Which gave it strength to pierce the guarded wit,
    And pass into the panting heart beneath
    With lightning and with music: the damp death
    Quenched its caress upon his icy lips;
    And, as a dying meteor stains a wreath
    Of moonlight vapour, which the cold night clips,
    It flushed through his pale limbs, and passed to its eclipse.

13. And others came . . . Desires and Adorations,
    Wingèd Persuasions and veiled Destinies,
    Splendours, and Glooms, and glimmering Incarnations
    Of hopes and fears, and twilight Phantasies;
    And Sorrow, with her family of Sighs,
    And Pleasure, blind with tears, led by the gleam
    Of her own dying smile instead of eyes,
    Came in slow pomp;—the moving pomp might seem
    Like pageantry of mist on an autumnal stream.

14. All he had loved, and moulded into thought,
    From shape, and hue, and odour, and sweet sound,
    Lamented Adonais. Morning sought
    Her eastern watch-tower, and her hair unbound,
    Wet with the tears which should adorn the ground,
    Dimmed the aërial eyes that kindle day;
    Afar the melancholy thunder moaned,
    Pale Ocean in unquiet slumber lay,
    And the wild winds flew round, sobbing in their dismay.

15. Lost Echo sits amid the voiceless mountains,
    And feeds her grief with his remembered lay,
    And will no more reply to winds or fountains,
    Or amorous birds perched on the young green spray,
    Or herdsman's horn, or bell at closing day,
    Since she can mimic not his lips, more dear
    Than those for whose disdain she pined away
    Into a shadow of all sounds:—a drear
    Murmur, between their songs, is all the woodmen hear.

16. Grief made the young Spring wild, and she threw down
    Her kindling buds, as if she Autumn were,
    Or they dead leaves; since her delight is flown,
    For whom should she have waked the sullen year?
    To Phoebus was not Hyacinth so dear
    Nor to himself Narcissus, as to both
    Thou, Adonais: wan they stand and sere
    Amid the faint companions of their youth,
    With dew all turned to tears; odour, to sighing ruth.

17. Thy spirit's sister, the lorn nightingale
    Mourns not her mate with such melodious pain;
    Not so the eagle, who like thee could scale
    Heaven, and could nourish in the sun's domain
    Her mighty youth with morning, doth complain,
    Soaring and screaming round her empty nest,
    As Albion wails for thee: the curse of Cain
    Light on his head who pierced thy innocent breast,
    And scared the angel soul that was its earthly guest!

18. Ah, woe is me! Winter is come and gone,
    But grief returns with the revolving year;
    The airs and streams renew their joyous tone;
    The ants, the bees, the swallows reappear;
    Fresh leaves and flowers deck the dead Season's bier;
    The amorous birds now pair in every brake,
    And build their mossy homes in field and brere;
    And the green lizard, and the golden snake,
    Like unimprisoned flames, out of their trance awake.

Through wood and stream and field and hill and Ocean
A quickening life from the Earth's heart has burst
As it has ever done, with change and motion,
From the great morning of the world when first
God dawned on Chaos; in its stream immersed,
The lamps of Heaven flash with a softer light;
All baser things pant with life's sacred thirst;
Diffuse themselves; and spend in love's delight
The beauty and the joy of their renewèd might.

The leprous corpse touched by this spirit tender
Exhales itself in flowers of gentle breath;
Like incarnations of the stars, when splendour
Is changed to fragrance, they illumine death
And mock the merry worm that wakes beneath;
Nought we know, dies. Shall that alone which knows
Be as a sword consumed before the sheath
By sightless lightning?—the intense atom glows
A moment, then is quenched in a most cold repose.

21. Alas! that all we loved of him should be,
    But for our grief, as if it had not been,
    And grief itself be mortal! Woe is me!
    Whence are we, and why are we? of what scene
    The actors or spectators? Great and mean
    Meet massed in death, who lends what life must
    [borrow.
    As long as skies are blue, and fields are green,
    Evening must usher night, night urge the morrow,
    Month follow month with woe, and year wake year to
    [sorrow.

22. *He* will awake no more, oh, never more!
    'Wake thou,' cried Misery, 'childless Mother, rise
    Out of thy sleep, and slake, in thy heart's core,
    A wound more fierce than his with tears and sighs.'
    And all the Dreams that watched Urania's eyes,
    And all the Echoes whom their sister's song
    Had held in holy silence, cried: 'Arise!'
    Swift as a Thought by the snake Memory stung,
    From her ambrosial rest the fading Splendour sprung.

23. She rose like an autumnal Night, that springs
    Out of the East, and follows wild and drear
    The golden Day, which, on eternal wings,
    Even as a ghost abandoning a bier,
    Has left the Earth a corpse. Sorrow and fear
    So struck, so roused, so rapt Urania;
    So saddened round her like an atmosphere
    Of stormy mist; so swept her on her way
    Even to the mournful place where Adonais lay.

24. Out of her secret Paradise she sped,
    Through camps and cities rough with stone, and steel,
    And human hearts, which to her aery tread
    Yielding not, wounded the invisible
    Palms of her tender feet where'er they fell:
    And barbèd tongues, and thoughts more sharp than
    Rent the soft Form they never could repel,   [they,
    Whose sacred blood, like the young tears of May,
    Paved with eternal flowers that undeserving way.

25. In the death-chamber for a moment Death,
    Shamed by the presence of that living Might,
    Blushed to annihilation, and the breath
    Revisited those lips, and life's pale light
    Flashed through those limbs, so late her dear delight.
    'Leave me not wild and drear and comfortless,
    As silent lightning leaves the starless night!
    Leave me not!' cried Urania: her distress
    Roused Death: Death rose and smiled, and met her vain
                                          ⌈caress.

26. 'Stay yet awhile! speak to me once again;
    Kiss me, so long but as a kiss may live;
    And in my heartless breast and burning brain
    That word, that kiss, shall all thoughts else survive,
    With food of saddest memory kept alive,
    Now thou art dead, as if it were a part
    Of thee, my Adonais! I would give
    All that I am to be as thou now art!
    But I am chained to Time, and cannot thence depart!

27. 'Oh gentle child, beautiful as thou wert,
    Why didst thou leave the trodden paths of men
    Too soon, and with weak hands though mighty heart
    Dare the unpastured dragon in his den?
    Defenceless as thou wert, oh where was then
    Wisdom the mirrored shield, or scorn the spear?
    Or hadst thou waited the full cycle, when
    Thy spirit should have filled its crescent sphere,
    The monsters of life's waste had fled from thee like deer.

28. 'The herded wolves, bold only to pursue;
    The obscene ravens, clamorous o'er the dead;
    The vultures to the conqueror's banner true
    Who feed where Desolation first has fed,
    And whose wings rain contagion;—how they fled,
    When like Apollo, from his golden bow,
    The Pythian of the age one arrow sped
    And smiled!—The spoilers tempt no second blow,
    They fawn on the proud feet that spurn them lying low.

29. 'The sun comes forth, and many reptiles spawn;
     He sets, and each ephemeral insect then
     Is gathered into death without a dawn,
     And the immortal stars awake again;
     So is it in the world of living men:
     A godlike mind soars forth, in its delight
     Making earth bare and veiling heaven, and when
     It sinks, the swarms that dimmed or shared its light
     Leave to its kindred lamps the spirit's awful night.'

30. Thus ceased she: and the mountain shepherds came,
     Their garlands sere, their magic mantles rent;
     The Pilgrim of Eternity, whose fame
     Over his living head like Heaven is bent,
     An early but enduring monument,
     Came, veiling all the lightnings of his song
     In sorrow; from her wilds Ierne sent
     The sweetest lyrist of her saddest wrong,
     And love taught grief to fall like music from his tongue.

31. Midst others of less note, came one frail Form,
    A phantom among men; companionless
    As the last cloud of an expiring storm
    Whose thunder is its knell; he, as I guess,
    Had gazed on Nature's naked loveliness,
    Actaeon-like, and now he fled astray
    With feeble steps o'er the world's wilderness,
    And his own thoughts, along that rugged way,
    Pursued, like raging hounds, their father and their prey.

32. A pardlike Spirit beautiful and swift—
    A Love in desolation masked;—a Power
    Girt round with weakness;—it can scarce uplift
    The weight of the superincumbent hour;
    It is a dying lamp, a falling shower,
    A breaking billow;—even whilst we speak
    Is it not broken? On the withering flower
    The killing sun smiles brightly: on a cheek
    The life can burn in blood, even while the heart may
    ⎡break.

33. His head was bound with pansies overblown,
    And faded violets, white, and pied, and blue;
    And a light spear topped with a cypress cone,
    Round whose rude shaft dark ivy tresses grew
    Yet dripping with the forest's noonday dew,
    Vibrated, as the ever-beating heart
    Shook the weak hand that grasped it; of that crew
    He came the last, neglected and apart;
    A herd-abandoned deer struck by the hunter's dart.

34. All stood aloof, and at his partial moan
    Smiled through their tears; well knew that gentle band
    Who in another's fate now wept his own—
    As in the accents of an unknown land
    He sung new sorrow; sad Urania scanned
    The Stranger's mien, and murmured: 'Who art thou?'
    He answered not, but with a sudden hand
    Made bare his branded and ensanguined brow,
    Which was like Cain's or Christ's—Oh! that it should
                                                   [be so!

35. What softer voice is hushed over the dead?
    Athwart what brow is that dark mantle thrown?
    What form leans sadly o'er the white death-bed,
    In mockery of monumental stone,
    The heavy heart heaving without a moan?
    If it be He, who gentlest of the wise,
    Taught, soothed, loved, honoured the departed one,
    Let me not vex, with inharmonious sighs,
    The silence of that heart's accepted sacrifice.

36. Our Adonais has drunk poison—oh!
    What deaf and viperous murderer could crown
    Life's early cup with such a draught of woe?
    The nameless worm would now itself disown:
    It felt, yet could escape, the magic tone
    Whose prelude held all envy, hate, and wrong,
    But what was howling in one breast alone,
    Silent with expectation of the song,
    Whose master's hand is cold, whose silver lyre unstrung.

37. Live thou, whose infamy is not thy fame!
    Live! fear no heavier chastisement from me,
    Thou noteless blot on a remembered name!
    But be thyself, and know thyself to be!
    And ever at thy season be thou free
    To spill the venom when thy fangs o'erflow:
    Remorse and Self-contempt shall cling to thee;
    Hot Shame shall burn upon thy secret brow,
    And like a beaten hound tremble thou shalt—as now.

38. Nor let us weep that our delight is fled
    Far from these carrion kites that scream below;
    He wakes or sleeps with the enduring dead;
    Thou canst not soar where he is sitting now.—
    Dust to the dust! but the pure spirit shall flow
    Back to the burning fountain whence it came,
    A portion of the Eternal, which must glow
    Through time and change, unquenchably the same,
    Whilst thy cold embers choke the sordid hearth of shame.

39. Peace, peace! he is not dead, he doth not sleep—
    He hath awakened from the dream of life—
    'Tis we, who lost in stormy visions, keep
    With phantoms an unprofitable strife,
    And in mad trance, strike with our spirit's knife
    Invulnerable nothings.—*We* decay
    Like corpses in a charnel; fear and grief
    Convulse us and consume us day by day,
    And cold hopes swarm like worms within our living
                                                    [clay.

40. He has outsoared the shadow of our night;
    Envy and calumny and hate and pain,
    And that unrest which men miscall delight,
    Can touch him not and torture not again;
    From the contagion of the world's slow stain
    He is secure, and now can never mourn
    A heart grown cold, a head grown grey in vain;
    Nor, when the spirit's self has ceased to burn,
    With sparkless ashes load an unlamented urn.

41. He lives, he wakes—'tis Death is dead, not he;
    Mourn not for Adonais.—Thou young Dawn
    Turn all thy dew to splendour, for from thee
    The spirit thou lamentest is not gone;
    Ye caverns and ye forests, cease to moan!
    Cease ye faint flowers and fountains, and thou Air
    Which like a mourning veil thy scarf hadst thrown
    O'er the abandoned Earth, now leave it bare
    Even to the joyous stars which smile on its despair!

42. He is made one with Nature: there is heard
    His voice in all her music, from the moan
    Of thunder, to the song of night's sweet bird;
    He is a presence to be felt and known
    In darkness and in light, from herb and stone,
    Spreading itself where'er that Power may move
    Which has withdrawn his being to its own;
    Which wields the world with never wearied love,
    Sustains it from beneath, and kindles it above.

43.   He is a portion of the loveliness
        Which once he made more lovely: he doth bear
        His part, while the one Spirit's plastic stress
        Sweeps through the dull dense world, compelling there
        All new successions to the forms they wear;
        Torturing th'unwilling dross that checks its flight
        To its own likeness, as each mass may bear;
        And bursting in its beauty and its might
        From trees and beasts and men into the Heavens' light.

44.   The splendours of the firmament of time
        May be eclipsed, but are extinguished not;
        Like stars to their appointed height they climb,
        And death is a low mist which cannot blot
        The brightness it may veil. When lofty thought
        Lifts a young heart above its mortal lair,
        And love and life contend in it, for what
        Shall be its earthly doom, the dead live there
        And move like winds of light on dark and stormy air.

45. The inheritors of unfulfilled renown
    Rose from their thrones, built beyond mortal thought,
    Far in the Unapparent. Chatterton
    Rose pale, his solemn agony had not
    Yet faded from him; Sidney as he fought
    And as he fell and as he lived and loved
    Sublimely mild, a Spirit without spot,
    Arose; and Lucan, by his death approved:
    Oblivion as they rose shrank like a thing reproved.

46. And many more, whose names on Earth are dark,
    But whose transmitted effluence cannot die
    So long as fire outlives the parent spark,
    Rose, robed in dazzling immortality.
    'Thou art become as one of us,' they cry,
    'It was for thee yon kingless sphere has long
    Swung blind in unascended majesty,
    Silent alone amid an Heaven of song.
    Assume thy wingèd throne, thou Vesper of our throng!'

47. Who mourns for Adonais? oh, come forth
     Fond wretch! and know thyself and him aright.
     Clasp with thy panting soul the pendulous Earth;
     As from a centre, dart thy spirit's light
     Beyond all worlds, until its spacious might
     Satiate the void circumference: then shrink
     Even to a point within our day and night;
     And keep thy heart light lest it make thee sink
     When hope has kindled hope, and lured thee to the
                                                    [brink;

48. Or go to Rome, which is the sepulchre,
     O, not of him, but of our joy: 'tis nought
     That ages, empires, and religions there
     Lie buried in the ravage they have wrought;
     For such as he can lend,—they borrow not
     Glory from those who made the world their prey;
     And he is gathered to the kings of thought
     Who waged contention with their time's decay,
     And of the past are all that cannot pass away.

49. Go thou to Rome,—at once the Paradise,
    The grave, the city, and the wilderness;
    And where its wrecks like shattered mountains rise,
    And flowering weeds, and fragrant copses dress
    The bones of Desolation's nakedness
    Pass, till the Spirit of the spot shall lead
    Thy footsteps to a slope of green access
    Where, like an infant's smile, over the dead,
    A light of laughing flowers along the grass is spread.

50. And grey walls moulder round, on which dull Time
    Feeds, like slow fire upon a hoary brand:
    And one keen pyramid with wedge sublime,
    Pavilioning the dust of him who planned
    This refuge for his memory, doth stand
    Like flame transformed to marble; and beneath,
    A field is spread, on which a newer band
    Have pitched in Heaven's smile their camp of death,
    Welcoming him we lose with scarce extinguished
                                        ⌈breath.

51. Here pause: these graves are all too young as yet
    To have outgrown the sorrow which consigned
    Its charge to each; and if the seal is set,
    Here, on one fountain of a mourning mind,
    Break it not thou! too surely shalt thou find
    Thine own well full, if thou returnest home,
    Of tears and gall. From the world's bitter wind
    Seek shelter in the shadow of the tomb.
    What Adonais is, why fear we to become?

52. The One remains, the many change and pass;
    Heaven's light forever shines, Earth's shadows fly;
    Life, like a dome of many-coloured glass,
    Stains the white radiance of Eternity,
    Until Death tramples it to fragments.—Die,
    If thou wouldst be with that which thou dost seek!
    Follow where all is fled!—Rome's azure sky,
    Flowers, ruins, statues, music, words, are weak
    The glory they transfuse with fitting truth to speak.

53. Why linger, why turn back, why shrink, my Heart?
    Thy hopes are gone before: from all things here
    They have departed; thou shouldst now depart!
    A light is passed from the revolving year,
    And man, and woman; and what still is dear
    Attracts to crush, repels to make thee wither.
    The soft sky smiles,—the low wind whispers near:
    'Tis Adonais calls! oh, hasten thither,
    No more let Life divide what Death can join together.

54. That Light whose smile kindles the Universe,
    That Beauty in which all things work and move,
    That Benediction which the eclipsing Curse
    Of birth can quench not, that sustaining Love
    Which through the web of being blindly wove
    By man and beast and earth and air and sea,
    Burns bright or dim, as each are mirrors of
    The fire for which all thirst, now beams on me,
    Consuming the last clouds of cold mortality.

55. The breath whose might I have invoked in song
     Descends on me; my spirit's bark is driven
     Far from the shore, far from the trembling throng
     Whose sails were never to the tempest given;
     The massy earth and spherèd skies are riven!
     I am borne darkly, fearfully, afar;
     Whilst burning through the inmost veil of Heaven,
     The soul of Adonais, like a star,
     Beacons from the abode where the Eternal are.

EPIPSYCHIDION

Sweet Spirit! Sister of that orphan one,
Whose empire is the name thou weepest on,
In my heart's temple I suspend to thee
These votive wreaths of withered memory.

Poor captive bird! who, from thy narrow cage,
Pourest such music, that it might assuage
The rugged hearts of those who prisoned thee,
Were they not deaf to all sweet melody;
This song shall be thy rose: its petals pale
Are dead, indeed, my adored Nightingale!
But soft and fragrant is the faded blossom,
And it has no thorn left to wound thy bosom.

High, spirit-wingèd Heart! who dost for ever
Beat thine unfeeling bars with vain endeavour,
Till those bright plumes of thought, in which arrayed
It over-soared this low and worldly shade,
Lie shattered; and thy panting, wounded breast
Stains with dear blood its unmaternal nest!
I weep vain tears: blood would less bitter be,
Yet poured forth gladlier, could it profit thee.

Seraph of Heaven! too gentle to be human,
Veiling beneath that radiant form of Woman
All that is unsupportable in thee
Of light, and love, and immortality!
Sweet Benediction in the eternal Curse!
Veiled Glory of this lampless Universe!
Thou Moon beyond the clouds! Thou living Form
Among the Dead! Thou Star above the Storm!
Thou Wonder, and thou Beauty, and thou Terror!
Thou Harmony of Nature's art! Thou Mirror
In whom, as in the splendour of the Sun,
All shapes look glorious which thou gazest on!
Ay, even the dim words which obscure thee now
Flash, lightning-like, with unaccustomed glow;
I pray thee that thou blot from this sad song
All of its much mortality and wrong
With those clear drops, which start like sacred dew
From the twin lights thy sweet soul darkens through,
Weeping, till sorrow becomes ecstasy:
Then smile on it, so that it may not die.

I never thought before my death to see
Youth's vision thus made perfect. Emily,
I love thee; though the world by no thin name
Will hide that love, from its unvalued shame.
Would we two had been twins of the same mother!
Or, that the name my heart lent to another

Could be a sister's bond for her and thee,
Blending two beams of one eternity!
Yet were one lawful and the other true,
These names, though dear, could paint not, as is due,
How beyond refuge I am thine. Ah me!
I am not thine: I am part of *thee*.

Sweet Lamp! my moth-like Muse has burnt its wings;
Or, like a dying swan who soars and sings,
Young Love should teach Time, in his own grey style,
All that thou art. Art thou not void of guile,
A lovely soul formed to be blest and bless?
A well of sealed and secret happiness,
Whose waters like blithe light and music are,
Vanquishing dissonance and gloom? A Star
Which moves not in the moving Heavens, alone?
A smile amid dark frowns? a gentle tone
Amid rude voices? a belovèd light?
A Solitude, a Refuge, a Delight?
A lute, which those whom love has taught to play
Make music on, to soothe the roughest day
And lull fond grief asleep? a buried treasure?
A cradle of young thoughts of wingless pleasure?
A violet-shrouded grave of Woe?—I measure
The world of fancies, seeking one like thee,
And find—alas! mine own infirmity.

She met me, Stranger, upon life's rough way,
And lured me towards sweet Death; as Night by Day,
Winter by Spring, or Sorrow by swift Hope,
Led into light, life, peace. An antelope,
In the suspended impulse of its lightness,
Were less æthereally light: the brightness
Of her divinest presence trembles through
Her limbs, as underneath a cloud of dew
Embodied in the windless Heaven of June
Amid the splendour-wingèd stars, the Moon
Burns, inextinguishably beautiful:
And from her lips, as from a hyacinth full
Of honey-dew, a liquid murmur drops,
Killing the sense with passion; sweet as stops
Of planetary music heard in trance.
In her mild lights the starry spirits dance,
The sun-beams of those wells which ever leap
Under the lightnings of the soul—too deep
For the brief fathom-line of thought or sense.
The glory of her being, issuing thence,
Stains the dead, blank, cold air with a warm shade
Of unentangled intermixture, made
By Love, of light and motion: one intense
Diffusion, one serene Omnipresence,
Whose flowing outlines mingle in their flowing,
Around her cheeks and utmost fingers glowing
With the unintermitted blood, which there

Quivers, (as in a fleece of snow-like air
The crimson pulse of living morning quiver,)
Continuously prolonged, and ending never,
Till they are lost, and in that Beauty furled
Which penetrates and clasps and fills the world;
Scarce visible from extreme loveliness.
Warm fragrance seems to fall from her light dress,
And her loose hair; and where some heavy tress
The air of her own speed has disentwined,
The sweetness seems to satiate the faint wind;
And in the soul a wild odour is felt,
Beyond the sense, like fiery dews that melt
Into the bosom of a frozen bud.—
See where she stands! a mortal shape indued
With love and life and light and deity,
And motion which may change but cannot die;
An image of some bright Eternity;
A shadow of some golden dream; a Splendour
Leaving the third sphere pilotless; a tender
Reflection of the eternal Moon of Love
Under whose motions life's dull billows move;
A Metaphor of Spring and Youth and Morning;
A Vision like incarnate April, warning,
With smiles and tears, Frost the Anatomy
Into his summer grave.
                                    Ah, woe is me!
What have I dared? where am I lifted? how

Shall I descend, and perish not? I know
That Love makes all things equal: I have heard
By mine own heart this joyous truth averred:
The spirit of the worm beneath the sod
In love and worship, blends itself with God.

Spouse! Sister! Angel! Pilot of the Fate
Whose course has been so starless! O too late
Belovèd! O too soon adored, by me!
For in the fields of immortality
My spirit should at first have worshipped thine,
A divine presence in a place divine;
Or should have moved beside it on this earth,
A shadow of that substance, from its birth;
But not as now:—I love thee; yes, I feel
That on the fountain of my heart a seal
Is set, to keep its waters pure and bright
For thee, since in those *tears* thou hast delight.
We—are we not formed, as notes of music are,
For one another, though dissimilar;
Such difference without discord, as can make
Those sweetest sounds in which all spirits shake
As trembling leaves in a continuous air?

Thy wisdom speaks in me, and bids me dare
Beacon the rocks on which high hearts are wrecked.
I never was attached to that great sect

Whose doctrine is, that each one should select
Out of the crowd a mistress or a friend,
And all the rest, though fair and wise, commend
To cold oblivion, though it is in the code
Of modern morals, and the beaten road
Which those poor slaves with weary footsteps tread,
Who travel to their home among the dead
By the broad highway of the world, and so
With one chained friend, perhaps a jealous foe,
The dreariest and the longest journey go.

True Love in this differs from gold and clay,
That to divide is not to take away.
Love is like understanding, that grows bright,
Gazing on many truths; 'tis like thy light,
Imagination! which from earth and sky,
And from the depths of human phantasy,
As from a thousand prisms and mirrors, fills
The Universe with glorious beams, and kills
Error, the worm, with many a sun-like arrow
Of its reverberated lightning. Narrow
The heart that loves, the brain that contemplates,
The life that wears, the spirit that creates
One object, and one form, and builds thereby
A sepulchre for its eternity.

Mind from its object differs most in this:
Evil from good; misery from happiness;
The baser from the nobler; the impure
And frail, from what is clear and must endure.
If you divide suffering and dross, you may
Diminish till it is consumed away;
If you divide pleasure and love and thought,
Each part exceeds the whole; and we know not
How much, while any yet remains unshared,
Of pleasure may be gained, of sorrow spared:
This truth is that deep well, whence sages draw
The unenvied light of hope; the eternal law
By which those live, to whom this world of life
Is as a garden ravaged, and whose strife
Tills for the promise of a later birth
The wilderness of this Elysian earth.

There was a Being whom my spirit oft
Met on its visioned wanderings, far aloft,
In the clear golden prime of my youth's dawn,
Upon the fairy isles of sunny lawn,
Amid the enchanted mountains, and the caves
Of divine sleep, and on the air-like waves
Of wonder-level dream, whose tremulous floor
Paved her light steps;—on an imagined shore,
Under the grey beak of some promontory
She met me, robed in such exceeding glory

That I beheld her not. In solitudes
Her voice came to me through the whispering woods,
And from the fountains, and the odours deep
Of flowers, which, like lips murmuring in their sleep
Of the sweet kisses which had lulled them there,
Breathed but of *her* to the enamoured air;
And from the breezes whether low or loud,
And from the rain of every passing cloud,
And from the singing of the summer-birds,
And from all sounds, all silence. In the words
Of antique verse and high romance,—in form
Sound, colour—in whatever checks that Storm
Which with the shattered present chokes the past;
And in that best philosophy, whose taste
Makes this cold common hell, our life, a doom
As glorious as a fiery martyrdom;
Her Spirit was the harmony of truth.—

    Then, from the caverns of my dreamy youth
I sprang, as one sandalled with plumes of fire,
And towards the lodestar of my one desire,
I flitted, like a dizzy moth, whose flight
Is as a dead leaf's in the owlet light,
When it would seek in Hesper's setting sphere
A radiant death, a fiery sepulchre,
As if it were a lamp of earthly flame.—
But She, whom prayers or tears then could not tame,

Passed, like a God throned on a wingèd planet,
Whose burning plumes to tenfold swiftness fan it,
Into the dreary cone of our life's shade;
And as a man with mighty loss dismayed,
I would have followed, though the grave between
Yawned like a gulf whose spectres are unseen:
When a voice said:—'O Thou of hearts the weakest,
The phantom is beside thee whom thou seekest.'
Then I—'Where?' the world's echo answered 'Where!'
And in that silence, and in my despair,
I questioned every tongueless wind that flew
Over my tower of mourning, if it knew
Whither 'twas fled, this soul out of my soul;
And murmured names and spells which have control
Over the sightless tyrants of our fate;
But neither prayer nor verse could dissipate
The night which closed on her; nor uncreate
That world within this Chaos, mine and me,
Of which she was the veiled Divinity,
The world I say of thoughts that worshipped her:
And therefore I went forth, with hope and fear
And every gentle passion sick to death,
Feeding my course with expectation's breath,
Into the wintry forest of our life;
And struggling through its error with vain strife,
And stumbling in my weakness and my haste,
And half bewildered by new forms, I passed

Seeking among those untaught foresters
If I could find one form resembling hers,
In which she might have masked herself from me.
There,—One, whose voice was venomed melody,
Sate by a well, under blue night-shade bowers;
The breath of her false mouth was like faint flowers,
Her touch was as electric poison,—flame
Out of her looks into my vitals came,
And from her living cheeks and bosom flew
A killing air, which pierced like honey-dew
Into the core of my green heart, and lay
Upon its leaves; until, as hair grown grey
O'er a young brow, they hid its unblown prime
With ruins of unseasonable time.

In many mortal forms I rashly sought
The shadow of that idol of my thought.
And some were fair—but beauty dies away:
Others were wise—but honeyed words betray:
And One was true—oh! why not true to me?
Then, as a hunted deer that could not flee,
I turned upon my thoughts, and stood at bay,
Wounded and weak and panting; the cold day
Trembled, for pity of my strife and pain;
When, like a noon-day dawn, there shone again
Deliverance. One stood on my path who seemed
As like the glorious shape which I had dreamed,

As is the Moon, whose changes ever run
Into themselves, to the eternal Sun;
The cold chaste Moon, the Queen of Heaven's bright
Who makes all beautiful on which she smiles;   [isles,
That wandering shrine of soft yet icy flame
Which ever is transformed, yet still the same,
And warms not but illumines. Young and fair
As the descended Spirit of that sphere,
She hid me, as the Moon may hide the night
From its own darkness, until all was bright
Between the Heaven and Earth of my calm mind,
And, as a cloud charioted by the wind,
She led me to a cave in that wild place,
And sate beside me, with her downward face
Illumining my slumbers, like the Moon
Waxing and waning o'er Endymion.
And I was laid asleep, spirit and limb,
And all my being became bright or dim
As the Moon's image in a summer sea,
According as she smiled or frowned on me;
And there I lay, within a chaste cold bed:
Alas, I then was nor alive nor dead:—
For at her silver voice came Death and Life,
Unmindful each of their accustomed strife,
Masked like twin babes, a sister and a brother,
The wandering hopes of one abandoned mother,
And through the cavern without wings they flew,

And cried 'Away, he is not of our crew.'
I wept, and though it be a dream, I weep.

    What storms then shook the ocean of my sleep,
Blotting that Moon, whose pale and waning lips
Then shrank as in the sickness of eclipse;—
And how my soul was as a lampless sea,
And who was then its Tempest; and when She,
The Planet of that hour, was quenched, what frost
Crept o'er those waters, till from coast to coast
The moving billows of my being fell
Into a death of ice, immoveable;—
And then—what earthquakes made it gape and split,
The white Moon smiling all the while on it,
These words conceal:—if not, each word would be
The key of staunchless tears. Weep not for me!

    At length, into the obscure Forest came
The Vision I had sought through grief and shame.
Athwart that wintry wilderness of thorns
Flashed from her motion splendour like the Morn's,
And from her presence life was radiated
Through the grey earth and branches bare and dead;
So that her way was paved, and roofed above
With flowers as soft as thoughts of budding love;
And music from her respiration spread
Like light,—all other sounds were penetrated

By the small, still, sweet spirit of that sound,
So that the savage winds hung mute around;
And odours warm and fresh fell from her hair
Dissolving the dull cold in the frore air:
Soft as an Incarnation of the Sun,
When light is changed to love, this glorious One
Floated into the cavern where I lay,
And called my Spirit, and the dreaming clay
Was lifted by the thing that dreamed below
As smoke by fire, and in her beauty's glow
I stood, and felt the dawn of my long night
Was penetrating me with living light:
I knew it was the Vision veiled from me
So many years—that it was Emily.

   Twin Spheres of light who rule this passive Earth,
This world of love, this *me*; and into birth
Awaken all its fruits and flowers, and dart
Magnetic might into its central heart;
And lift its billows and its mists, and guide
By everlasting laws, each wind and tide
To its fit cloud, and its appointed cave;
And lull its storms, each in the craggy grave
Which was its cradle, luring to faint bowers
The armies of the rainbow-wingèd showers;
And, as those married lights, which from the towers
Of Heaven look forth and fold the wandering globe

In liquid sleep and splendour, as a robe;
And all their many-mingled influence blend,
If equal, yet unlike, to one sweet end;—
So ye, bright regents, with alternate sway
Govern my sphere of being, night and day!
Thou, not disdaining even a borrowed might;
Thou, not eclipsing a remoter light;
And, through the shadow of the seasons three,
From Spring to Autumn's sere maturity,
Light it into the Winter of the tomb,
Where it may ripen to a brighter bloom.
Thou too, O Comet beautiful and fierce,
Who drew the heart of this frail Universe
Towards thine own; till, wrecked in that convulsion,
Alternating attraction and repulsion,
Thine went astray and that was rent in twain;
Oh, float into our azure heaven again!
Be there love's folding-star at thy return;
The living Sun will feed thee from its urn
Of golden fire; the Moon will veil her horn
In thy last smiles; adoring Even and Morn
Will worship thee with incense of calm breath
And lights and shadows; as the star of Death
And Birth is worshipped by those sisters wild
Called Hope and Fear—upon the heart are piled
Their offerings,—of this sacrifice divine
A World shall be the altar.

Lady mine,
Scorn not these flowers of thought, the fading birth
Which from its heart of hearts that plant puts forth
Whose fruit, made perfect by thy sunny eyes,
Will be as of the trees of Paradise.

The day is come, and thou wilt fly with me.
To whatsoe'er of dull mortality
Is mine, remain a vestal sister still;
To the intense, the deep, the imperishable,
Not mine but me, henceforth be thou united
Even as a bride, delighting and delighted.
The hour is come:—the destined Star has risen
Which shall descend upon a vacant prison.
The walls are high, the gates are strong, thick set
The sentinels—but true love never yet
Was thus constrained: it overleaps all fence:
Like lightning, with invisible violence
Piercing its continents; like Heaven's free breath,
Which he who grasps can hold not; liker Death,
Who rides upon a thought, and makes his way
Through temple, tower, and palace, and the array
Of arms: more strength has Love than he or they;
For it can burst his charnel, and make free
The limbs in chains, the heart in agony,
The soul in dust and chaos.
                    Emily,

A ship is floating in the harbour now,
A wind is hovering o'er the mountain's brow;
There is a path on the sea's azure floor,
No keel has ever ploughed that path before;
The halcyons brood around the foamless isles;
The treacherous Ocean has forsworn its wiles;
The merry mariners are bold and free:
Say, my heart's sister, wilt thou sail with me?
Our bark is as an albatross, whose nest
Is a far Eden of the purple East;
And we between her wings will sit, while Night
And Day, and Storm, and Calm, pursue their flight,
Our ministers, along the boundless Sea,
Treading each other's heels, unheededly.
It is an isle under Ionian skies,
Beautiful as a wreck of Paradise,
And, for the harbours are not safe and good,
This land would have remained a solitude
But for some pastoral people native there,
Who from the Elysian, clear, and golden air
Draw the last spirit of the age of gold,
Simple and spirited; innocent and bold.
The blue Aegean girds this chosen home,
With ever-changing sound and light and foam
Kissing the sifted sands, and caverns hoar;
And all the winds wandering along the shore
Undulate with the undulating tide:

There are thick woods where sylvan forms abide;
And many a fountain, rivulet, and pond,
As clear as elemental diamond,
Or serene morning air; and far beyond,
The mossy tracks made by the goats and deer
(Which the rough shepherd treads but once a year,)
Pierce into glades, caverns, and bowers, and halls
Built round with ivy, which the waterfalls
Illumining, with sound that never fails
Accompany the noon-day nightingales;
And all the place is peopled with sweet airs;
The light clear element which the isle wears
Is heavy with the scent of lemon-flowers,
Which floats like mist laden with unseen showers,
And falls upon the eye-lids like faint sleep;
And from the moss violets and jonquils peep,
And dart their arrowy odour through the brain
Till you might faint with that delicious pain;
And every motion, odour, beam, and tone,
With that deep music is in unison,
Which is a soul within the soul—they seem
Like echoes of an antenatal dream.—
It is an isle 'twixt Heaven, Air, Earth, and Sea
Cradled, and hung in clear tranquillity;
Bright as that wandering Eden Lucifer,
Washed by the soft blue Oceans of young air.
It is a favoured place. Famine or Blight,

Pestilence, War and Earthquake, never light
Upon its mountain-peaks; blind vultures, they
Sail onward far upon their fatal way:
The wingèd storms, chaunting their thunder-psalm
To other lands, leave azure chasms of calm
Over this isle or weep themselves in dew,
From which its fields and woods ever renew
Their green and golden immortality.
And from the sea there rise, and from the sky
There fall, clear exhalations, soft and bright,
Veil after veil, each hiding some delight,
Which Sun or Moon or zephyr draw aside,
Till the isle's beauty, like a naked bride
Glowing at once with love and loveliness,
Blushes and trembles at its own excess:
Yet, like a buried lamp, a Soul no less
Burns in the heart of this delicious isle,
An atom of th'Eternal, whose own smile
Unfolds itself, and may be felt not seen
O'er the grey rocks, blue waves, and forests green,
Filling their bare and void interstices.—
But the chief marvel of the wilderness
Is a lone dwelling, built by whom or how
None of the rustic island-people know:
'Tis not a tower of strength, though with its height
It overtops the woods; but, for delight,
Some wise and tender Ocean-King, ere crime

Had been invented, in the world's young prime,
Reared it, a wonder of that simple time,
An envy of the isles, a pleasure-house
Made sacred to his sister and his spouse.
It scarce seems now a wreck of human art,
But as it were Titanic; in the heart
Of Earth having assumed its form, then grown
Out of the mountain, from the living stone,
Lifting itself in caverns light and high:
For all the antique and learnèd imagery
Has been erased, and in the place of it
The ivy and the wild-vine interknit
The volumes of their many-twining stems;
Parasite flowers illume with dewy gems
The lampless halls, and when they fade, the sky
Peeps through their winter-woof of tracery
With Moon-light patches, or star atoms keen,
Or fragments of the day's intense serene,—
Working mosaic on their Parian floors.
And, day and night, aloof, from the high towers
And terraces, the Earth and Ocean seem
To sleep in one another's arms, and dream
Of waves, flowers, clouds, woods, rocks, and all that we
Read in their smiles, and call reality.

This isle and house are mine, and I have vowed
Thee to be lady of the solitude.—
And I have fitted up some chambers there
Looking towards the golden Eastern air,
And level with the living winds, which flow
Like waves above the living waves below.—
I have sent books and music there, and all
Those instruments with which high spirits call
The future from its cradle, and the past
Out of its grave, and make the present last
In thoughts and joys which sleep, but cannot die,
Folded within their own eternity.
Our simple life wants little, and true taste
Hires not the pale drudge Luxury, to waste
The scene it would adorn, and therefore still,
Nature, with all her children, haunts the hill.
The ring-dove, in the embowering ivy, yet
Keeps up her love-lament, and the owls flit
Round the evening tower, and the young stars glance
Between the quick bats in their twilight dance;
The spotted deer bask in the fresh moon-light
Before our gate, and the slow, silent night
Is measured by the pants of their calm sleep.
Be this our home in life, and when years heap
Their withered hours, like leaves, on our decay,
Let us become the over-hanging day,
The living soul of this Elysian isle,

Conscious, inseparable, one. Meanwhile
We two will rise, and sit, and walk together,
Under the roof of blue Ionian weather,
And wander in the meadows, or ascend
The mossy mountains, where the blue heavens bend
With lightest winds, to touch their paramour;
Or linger, where the pebble-paven shore,
Under the quick, faint kisses of the sea
Trembles and sparkles as with ecstasy,—
Possessing and possessed by all that is
Within that calm circumference of bliss,
And by each other, till to love and live
Be one:—or, at the noontide hour, arrive
Where some old cavern hoar seems yet to keep
The moonlight of the expired night asleep,
Through which the awakened day can never peep;
A veil for our seclusion, close as Night's,
Where secure sleep may kill thine innocent lights;
Sleep, the fresh dew of languid love, the rain
Whose drops quench kisses till they burn again.
And we will talk, until thought's melody
Become too sweet for utterance, and it die
In words, to live again in looks, which dart
With thrilling tone into the voiceless heart,
Harmonizing silence without a sound.
Our breath shall intermix, our bosoms bound,
And our veins beat together; and our lips

With other eloquence than words, eclipse
The soul that burns between them and the wells
Which boil under our being's inmost cells,
The fountains of our deepest life, shall be
Confused in passion's golden purity,
As mountain-springs under the morning Sun.
We shall become the same, we shall be one
Spirit within two frames, oh! wherefore two?
One passion in twin-hearts, which grows and grew,
Till, like two meteors of expanding flame,
Those spheres instinct with it become the same,
Touch, mingle, are transfigured; ever still
Burning, yet ever inconsumable:
In one another's substance finding food,
Like flames too pure and light and unimbued
To nourish their bright lives with baser prey,
Which point to Heaven and cannot pass away:
One hope within two wills, one will beneath
Two overshadowing minds, one life, one death,
One Heaven, one Hell, one immortality,
And one annihilation. Woe is me!
The wingèd words on which my soul would pierce
Into the height of love's rare Universe,
Are chains of lead around its flight of fire.—
I pant, I sink, I tremble, I expire!

TO JANE: THE RECOLLECTION

I

Now the last day of many days,
    All beautiful and bright as thou,
        The loveliest and the last, is dead,
Rise, Memory, and write its praise!
    Up,—to thy wonted work! come, trace
        The epitaph of glory fled,—
For now the Earth has changed its face,
    A frown is on the Heaven's brow.

II

We wandered to the Pine Forest
    That skirts the Ocean's foam,
The lightest wind was in its nest,
    The tempest in its home.
The whispering waves were half asleep,
    The clouds were gone to play,
And on the bosom of the deep
    The smile of Heaven lay;
It seemed as if the hour were one
    Sent from beyond the skies,
Which scattered from above the sun
    A light of Paradise.

III

We paused amid the pines that stood
　　The giants of the waste,
Tortured by storms to shapes as rude
　　As serpents interlaced,
And soothed by every azure breath,
　　That under Heaven is blown,
To harmonies and hues beneath,
　　As tender as its own;
Now all the tree-tops lay asleep,
　　Like green waves on the sea,
As still as in the silent deep
　　The ocean woods may be.

IV

How calm it was!—the silence there
　　By such a chain was bound
That even the busy woodpecker
　　Made stiller by her sound
The inviolable quietness;
　　The breath of peace we drew
With its soft motion made not less
　　The calm that round us grew.
There seemed from the remotest seat
　　Of the white mountain waste,

To the soft flower beneath our feet,
    A magic circle traced,—
A spirit interfused around,
    A thrilling, silent life,—
To momentary peace it bound
    Our mortal nature's strife;
And still I felt the centre of
    The magic circle there
Was one fair form that filled with love
    The lifeless atmosphere.

                    V
We paused beside the pools that lie
    Under the forest bough,—
Each seemed as 'twere a little sky
    Gulfed in a world below;
A firmament of purple light
    Which in the dark earth lay,
More boundless than the depth of night,
    And purer than the day—
In which the lovely forests grew,
    As in the upper air,
More perfect both in shape and hue
    Than any spreading there.
There lay the glade and neighbouring lawn,
    And through the dark green wood
The white sun twinkling like the dawn

Out of a speckled cloud.
Sweet views which in our world above
    Can never well be seen,
Were imagined by the water's love
    Of that fair forest green.
And all was interfused beneath
    With an Elysian glow,
An atmosphere without a breath,
    A softer day below.
Like one beloved the scene had lent
    To the dark water's breast,
Its every leaf and lineament
    With more than truth expressed;
Until an envious wind crept by,
    Like an unwelcome thought,
Which from the mind's too faithful eye
    Blots one dear image out.
Though thou art ever fair and kind,
    The forests ever green,
Less oft is peace in Shelley's mind,
    Than calm in waters, seen.

LETTER TO MARIA GISBORNE

The spider spreads her webs, whether she be
In poet's tower, cellar or barn or tree;
The silk-worm in the dark green mulberry leaves
His winding sheet and cradle ever weaves;
So I, a thing whom moralists call worm,
Sit spinning still round this decaying form
From the fine threads of rare and subtle thought—
No net of words in garish colours wrought
To catch the idle buzzers of the day—
But a soft cell where, when that fades away,
Memory may clothe in wings my living name
And feed it with the asphodels of fame,
Which in those hearts that must remember me
Grow, making love an immortality.

Whoever should behold me now, I wist,
Would think I were a mighty mechanist,
Bent with sublime Archimedean art
To breathe a soul into the iron heart
Of some machine portentous, or strange gin,
Which, by the force of figured spells, might win
Its way over the sea, and sport therein;
For round the walls are hung dread engines, such
As Vulcan never wrought for Jove to clutch
Ixion or the Titans;—or the quick

Wit of that man of God, St. Dominic,
To convince Atheist, Turk or heretic;
Or those in philanthropic council met
Who thought to pay some interest for the debt
They owed to Jesus Christ for their salvation,
By giving a faint foretaste of damnation
To Shakespeare, Sidney, Spenser, and the rest
Who made our land an island of the blest,
When lamplike Spain, who now relumes her fire
On Freedom's hearth, grew dim with Empire—
With thumbscrews, wheels, with tooth and spike and
Which fishers found under the utmost crag   [jag,
Of Cornwall, and the storm-encompassed isles,
Where to the sky the rude sea rarely smiles
Unless in treacherous wrath, as on the morn
When the exulting elements, in scorn,
Satiated with destroyed destruction, lay
Sleeping in beauty on their mangled prey,
As panthers sleep;—and other strange and dread
Magical forms the brick floor overspread—
Proteus transformed to metal did not make
More figures or more strange; nor did he take
Such shapes of unintelligible brass,
Or heap himself in such a horrid mass
Of tin and iron not to be understood,
And forms of unimaginable wood,
To puzzle Tubal Cain and all his brood:

Great screws, and cones, and wheels, and groovèd
The elements of what will stand the shocks   [blocks,
Of wave and wind and time.—Upon the table
More knacks and quips there be than I am able
To catalogize in this verse of mine:—
A pretty bowl of wood, not full of wine
But quicksilver, that dew which the gnomes drink
When at their subterranean toil they swink,
Pledging the demons of the earthquake, who
Reply to them in lava, cry halloo!
And call out to the cities o'er their head—
Roofs, towers, and shrines, the dying and the dead,
Crash through the chinks of earth—and then all quaff
Another rouse, and hold their ribs and laugh.
This quicksilver no gnome has drunk—within
The walnut bowl it lies, veinèd and thin,
In colour like the wake of light that stains
The Tuscan deep, when from the moist moon rains
The inmost shower of its white fire—the breeze
Is still—blue heaven smiles over the pale seas.
And in this bowl of quicksilver—for I
Yield to the impulse of an infancy
Outlasting manhood—I have made to float
A rude idealism of a paper boat:
A hollow screw with cogs—Henry will know
The thing I mean, and laugh at me, if so
He fears not I should do more mischief—next

Lie bills and calculations much perplexed,
With steam boats, frigates and machinery quaint
Traced over them in blue and yellow paint.
Then comes a range of mathematical
Instruments, for plans nautical and statical;
A heap of rosin, a queer broken glass
With ink in it; a china cup that was
What it will never be again, I think,
A thing from which sweet lips were wont to drink
The liquor doctors rail at—and which I
Will quaff in spite of them—and when we die
We'll toss up who died first of drinking tea,
And cry out, 'Heads or tails?' where'er we be.
Near that a dusty paint box, some odd hooks,
A half-burnt match, an ivory block, three books
Where conic sections, spherics, logarithms,
To great Laplace from Saunderson and Sims
Lie heaped in their harmonious disarray
Of figures—disentangle them who may.
Baron de Tott's memoirs beside them lie,
And some odd volumes of old chemistry.
Near those a most inexplicable tin thing
With lead in the middle—I'm conjecturing
How to make Henry understand—but no,
I'll leave, as Spenser says, with many mo,
This secret in the pregnant womb of time,
Too vast a matter for so weak a rhyme.

And here like some weird Archimage sit I,
Plotting dark spells and devilish enginery,
The self-impelling steam wheels of the mind
Which pump up oaths from clergymen, and grind
The gentle spirit of our meek reviews
Into a powdery foam of salt abuse,
Ruffling the dull wave of their self-content—
I sit, and smile or sigh, as is my bent,
But not for them—Libeccio rushes round
With an inconstant and an idle sound,
I heed him more than them—the thundersmoke
Is gathering on the mountains, like a cloak
Folded athwart their shoulders broad and bare;
The ripe corn under the undulating air
Undulates like an ocean;—and the vines
Are trembling wide in all their trellised lines—
The murmur of the awakening sea doth fill
The empty pauses of the blast—the hill
Looks hoary through the white electric rain—
And from the glens beyond, in sullen strain
The interrupted thunder howls; above
One chasm of heaven smiles, like the eye of Love,
O'er the unquiet world;—while such things are,
How could one worth your friendship heed this war
Of worms? the shriek of the world's carrion jays,
Their censure, or their wonder, or their praise?

You are not here!...the quaint witch Memory sees
In vacant chairs your absent images,
And points where once you sat, and now should be
But are not—I demand if ever we
Shall meet as then we met,—and she replies,
Veiling in awe her second-sighted eyes,
'I know the past alone—but summon home
My sister Hope,—she speaks of all to come.'
But I, an old diviner, who know well
Every false verse of that sweet oracle,
Turned to the sad enchantress once again,
And sought a respite from my gentle pain
In citing every passage o'er and o'er
Of our communion—how on the sea shore
We watched the ocean and the sky together
Under the roof of blue Italian weather;
How I ran home through last year's thunderstorm,
And felt the transverse lightning linger warm
Upon my cheek—and how we often made
Feasts for each other, where good will outweighed
The frugal luxury of our country cheer,
As well it might, were it less firm and clear
Than ours must ever be;—and how we spun
A shroud of talk to hide us from the sun
Of this familiar life, which seems to be
But is not,—or is but quaint mockery
Of all we would believe; or sadly blame

The jarring and inexplicable frame
Of this wrong world—and then anatomize
The purposes and thoughts of men whose eyes
Were closed in distant years—or widely guess
The issue of the earth's great business,.
When we shall be, as we no longer are,
Like babbling gossips safe, who hear the war
Of winds, and sigh, but tremble not—or how
You listened to some interrupted flow
Of visionary rhyme, in joy and pain
Struck from the inmost fountains of my brain
With little skill perhaps—or how we sought
Those deepest wells of passion and of thought
Wrought by wise poets in the waste of years,
Staining their sacred waters with our tears,
Quenching a thirst ever to be renewed!
Or how I, wisest lady! then indued
The language of a land which now is free
And winged with thoughts of truth and majesty
Flits round the tyrant's sceptre like a cloud,
And bursts the peopled prisons, cries aloud
'My name is Legion!'—that majestic tongue
Which Calderon over the desert flung
Of ages and of nations; and which found
An echo in our hearts, and with the sound
Startled oblivion;—thou wert then to me
As is a nurse, when inarticulately

A child would talk as its grown parents do.
If living winds the rapid clouds pursue,
If hawks chase doves through the aethereal way,
Huntsmen the innocent deer, and beasts their prey,
Why should not we rouse with the spirit's blast
Out of the forest of the pathless past
These recollected pleasures?
                                                You are now
In London, that great sea, whose ebb and flow
At once is deaf and loud, and on the shore
Vomits its wrecks, and still howls on for more.
Yet in its depth what treasures!—You will see
That which was Godwin,—greater none than he
Though fallen—and fallen on evil times—to stand
Among the spirits of our age and land,
Before the dread tribunal of *to come*
The foremost—while Rebuke covers, pale and dumb.
You will see Coleridge—he who sits obscure
In the exceeding lustre and the pure
Intense irradiation of a mind,
Which, with its own internal lightning blind,
Flags wearily through darkness and despair—
A cloud-encircled meteor of the air,
A hooded eagle among blinking owls.—
You will see Hunt—one of those happy souls
Who are the salt of the earth, and without whom
This world would smell like what it is—a tomb;

Who is, what others seem;—his room no doubt
Is still adorned with many a cast from Shout,
With graceful flowers, tastefully placed about;
And coronals of bay from ribbons hung,
And brighter wreaths in neat disorder flung,
The gifts of the most learn'd among some dozens
Of female friends, sisters-in-law and cousins.
And there is he with his eternal puns,
Which beat the dullest brain for smiles, like duns
Thundering for money at a poet's door;
Alas, it is no use to say 'I'm poor!'
Or oft in graver mood, when he will look
Things wiser than were ever read in book,
Except in Shakespeare's wisest tenderness.—
You will see Hogg—and I cannot express
His virtues, though I know that they are great,
Because he locks, then barricades, the gate
Within which they inhabit;—of his wit
And wisdom, you'll cry out when you are bit.
He is a pearl within an oyster shell,
One of the richest of the deep. And there
Is English Peacock with his mountain Fair,
Turned into a Flamingo,—that shy bird
That gleams i' the Indian air. Have you not heard
When a man marries, dies, or turns Hindoo,
His best friends hear no more of him?—but you
Will see him and will like him too, I hope,

With the milk-white Snowdonian Antelope
Matched with this Cameleopard.—His fine wit
Makes such a wound, the knife is lost in it;
A strain too learnèd for a shallow age,
Too wise for selfish bigots; let his page
Which charms the chosen spirits of the time
Fold itself up for the serener clime
Of years to come, and find its recompense
In that just expectation.—Wit and sense,
Virtue and human knowledge, all that might
Make this dull world a business of delight,
Are all combined in Horace Smith.—And these,
With some exceptions which I need not tease
Your patience by descanting on, are all
You and I know in London—

                      I recall
My thoughts, and bid you look upon the night.
As water does a sponge, so the moonlight
Fills the void, hollow, universal air—
What see you?—unpavilioned heaven is fair,
Whether the moon, into her chamber gone,
Leaves midnight to the golden stars, or wan
Climbs with diminished beams the azure steep;
Or whether clouds sail o'er the inverse deep,
Piloted by the many-wandering blast,
And the rare stars rush through them dim and fast:—
All this is beautiful in every land.—

But what see you beside?—a shabby stand
Of hackney coaches—a brick house or wall
Fencing some lordly court, white with the scrawl
Of our unhappy politics; or worse—
A wretched woman reeling by, whose curse
Mixed with the watchman's, partner of her trade,
You must accept in place of serenade—
Or yellow-haired Pollonia murmuring
To Henry some unutterable thing.—
I see a chaos of green leaves and fruit
Built round dark caverns, even to the root
Of the living stems which feed them—in whose bowers
There sleep in their dark dew the folded flowers;
Beyond, the surface of the unsickled corn
Trembles not in the slumbering air, and borne
In circles quaint, and ever-changing dance,
Like wingèd stars the fire-flies flash and glance
Pale in the open moonshine, but each one
Under the dark trees seems a little sun,
A meteor tamed, a fixed star gone astray
From the silver regions of the Milky Way;—
Afar the Contadino's song is heard,
Rude, but made sweet by distance—and a bird
Which cannot be the nightingale, and yet
I know none else that sings so sweet as it
At this late hour;—and then all is still—
Now, Italy or London—which you will!

Next winter you must pass with me; I'll have
My house by that time turned into a grave
Of dead despondence and low-thoughted care,
And all the dreams which our tormentors are.
Oh, that Hunt, Hogg, Peacock and Smith were there,
With every thing belonging to them fair!
We will have books, Spanish, Italian, Greek;
And ask one week to make another week
As like his father as I'm unlike mine,
Which is not his fault, as you may divine.
Though we eat little flesh and drink no wine,
Yet let's be merry: we'll have tea and toast,
Custards for supper, and an endless host
Of syllabubs and jellies and mince-pies,
And other such lady-like luxuries—
Feasting on which, we will philosophize!
And we'll have fires out of the Grand Duke's wood
To thaw the six weeks' winter in our blood.
And then we'll talk;—what shall we talk about?
Oh! there are themes enough for many a bout
Of thought-entangled descant;—as to nerves,
With cones and parallelograms and curves
I've sworn to strangle them if once they dare
To bother me—when you are with me there,
And they shall never more sip laudanum
From Helicon or Himeros:—well, come,
And in despite of God and of the devil,

We'll make our friendly philosophic revel
Outlast the leafless time;—till buds and flowers
Warn the obscure inevitable hours
Sweet meeting by sad parting to renew—
'Tomorrow to fresh woods and pastures new.'

From PROMETHEUS UNBOUND

From Act One   The Earth
Ere Babylon was dust,
The Magus Zoroaster, my dead child,
Met his own image walking in the garden.
That apparition, sole of men, he saw.
For know there are two worlds of life and death:
One that which thou beholdest; but the other
Is underneath the grave, where do inhabit
The shadows of all forms that think and live
Till death unite them and they part no more;
Dreams and the light imaginings of men,
And all that faith creates or love desires,
Terrible, strange, sublime and beauteous shapes.
There thou art, and dost hang, a writhing shade,
'Mid whirlwind-peopled mountains; all the gods
Are there, and all the powers of nameless worlds,

Vast, sceptred phantoms; heroes, men, and beasts;
And Demogorgon, a tremendous gloom;
And he, the supreme Tyrant, on his throne
Of burning gold. Son, one of these shall utter
The curse which all remember. Call at will
Thine own ghost, or the ghost of Jupiter,
Hades or Typhon, or what mightier Gods
From all-prolific Evil, since thy ruin
Have sprung, and trampled on my prostrate sons.
Ask, and they must reply: so the revenge
Of the Supreme may sweep through vacant shades,
As rainy wind through the abandoned gate
Of a fallen palace.

From PROMETHEUS UNBOUND

From Act One   Chorus of Spirits
From unremembered ages we
Gentle guides and guardians be
Of heaven-oppressed mortality;
And we breathe, and sicken not,
The atmosphere of human thought:
Be it dim, and dank, and gray,
Like a storm-extinguished day,
Travelled o'er by dying gleams;
   Be it bright as all between
Cloudless skies and windless streams,
   Silent, liquid, and serene;
As the birds within the wind,
   As the fish within the wave,
As the thoughts of man's own mind
   Float through all above the grave;
We make there our liquid lair,
Voyaging cloudlike and unpent
Through the boundless element:
Thence we bear the prophecy
Which begins and ends in thee!
   Ione. More yet come, one by one: the air around them
Looks radiant as the air around a star.

First Spirit
On a battle-trumpet's blast
I fled hither, fast, fast, fast,
'Mid the darkness upward cast.
From the dust of creeds outworn,
From the tyrant's banner torn,
Gathering 'round me, onward borne,
There was mingled many a cry—
Freedom! Hope! Death! Victory!
Till they faded through the sky;
And one sound, above, around,
One sound beneath, around, above,
Was moving; 'twas the soul of Love;
'Twas the hope, the prophecy,
Which begins and ends in thee.

Second Spirit

A rainbow's arch stood on the sea,
Which rocked beneath, immovably;
And the triumphant storm did flee,
Like a conqueror, swift and proud,
Between, with many a captive cloud,
A shapeless, dark and rapid crowd,
Each by lightning riven in half:
I heard the thunder hoarsely laugh:
Mighty fleets were strewn like chaff
And spread beneath a hell of death
O'er the white waters. I alit
On a great ship lightning-split,
And speeded hither on the sigh
Of one who gave an enemy
His plank, then plunged aside to die.

Third Spirit
I sate beside a sage's bed,
And the lamp was burning red
Near the book where he had fed,
When a Dream with plumes of flame
To his pillow hovering came,
And I knew it was the same
Which had kindled long ago
Pity, eloquence, and woe;
And the world awhile below
Wore the shade, its lustre made.
It has borne me here as fleet
As Desire's lightning feet:
I must ride it back ere morrow,
Or the sage will wake in sorrow.

Fourth Spirit

On a poet's lips I slept
Dreaming like a love-adept
In the sound his breathing kept;
Nor seeks nor finds he mortal blisses,
But feeds on the aëreal kisses
Of shapes that haunt thought's wildernesses.
He will watch from dawn to gloom
The lake-reflected sun illume
The yellow bees in the ivy-bloom,
Nor heed nor see, what things they be;
But from these create he can
Forms more real than living man,
Nurslings of immortality!
One of these awakened me,
And I sped to succour thee.

From PROMETHEUS UNBOUND

From Act Two   Asia

Who reigns? There was the Heaven and Earth at first,
And Light and Love; then Saturn, from whose throne
Time fell, an envious shadow: such the state
Of the earth's primal spirits beneath his sway,
As the calm joy of flowers and living leaves
Before the wind or sun has withered them
And semivital worms; but he refused
The birthright of their being, knowledge, power,
The skill which wields the elements, the thought
Which pierces this dim universe like light,
Self-empire, and the majesty of love;
For thirst of which they fainted. Then Prometheus
Gave wisdom, which is strength, to Jupiter,
And with this law alone, 'Let man be free,'
Clothed him with the dominion of wide Heaven.
To know nor faith, nor love, nor law; to be
Omnipotent but friendless is to reign;
And Jove now reigned: for on the race of man
First famine, and then toil, and then disease,
Strife, wounds, and ghastly death unseen before,
Fell; and the unseasonable seasons drove
With alternating shafts of frost and fire,
Their shelterless, pale tribes to mountain caves:
And in their desert hearts fierce wants he sent,

And mad disquietudes, and shadows idle
Of unreal good, which levied mutual war,
So ruining the lair wherein they raged.
Prometheus saw, and waked the legioned hopes
Which sleep within folded Elysian flowers,
Nepenthe, Moly, Amaranth, fadeless blooms,
That they might hide with thin and rainbow wings
The shape of Death; and Love he sent to bind
The disunited tendrils of that vine
Which bears the wine of life, the human heart;
And he tamed fire which, like some beast of prey,
Most terrible, but lovely, played beneath
The frown of man; and tortured to his will
Iron and gold, the slaves and signs of power,
And gems and poisons, and all subtlest forms
Hidden beneath the mountains and the waves.
He gave man speech, and speech created thought,
Which is the measure of the universe;
And Science struck the thrones of earth and heaven,
Which shook, but fell not; and the harmonious mind
Poured itself forth in all-prophetic song;
And music lifted up the listening spirit
Until it walked, exempt from mortal care.
Godlike, o'er the clear billows of sweet sound;
And human hands first mimicked and then mocked,
With moulded limbs more lovely than its own,
The human form, till marble grew divine;

And mothers, gazing, drank the love men see
Reflected in their race, behold, and perish.
He told the hidden power of herbs and springs,
And Disease drank and slept. Death grew like sleep.
He taught the implicated orbits woven
Of the wide-wandering stars; and how the sun
Changes his lair, and by what secret spell
The pale moon is transformed, when her broad eye
Gazes not on the interlunar sea:
He taught to rule, as life directs the limbs,
The tempest-wingèd chariots of the Ocean,
And the Celt knew the Indian. Cities then
Were built, and through their snow-like columns flowed
The warm winds, and the azure aether shone,
And the blue sea and shadowy hills were seen.
Such, the alleviations of his state,
Prometheus gave to man, for which he hangs
Withering in destined pain: but who rains down
Evil, the immedicable plague, which, while
Man looks on his creation like a God
And sees that it is glorious, drives him on,
The wreck of his own will, the scorn of earth,
The outcast, the abandoned, the alone?
Not Jove: while yet his frown shook Heaven, ay, when
His adversary from adamantine chains
Cursed him, he trembled like a slave. Declare
Who is his master? Is he too a slave?

From PROMETHEUS UNBOUND

From Act Three · *Spirit of the Hour*

Soon as the sound had ceased whose thunder filled
The abysses of the sky and the wide earth,
There was a change: the impalpable thin air
And the all-circling sunlight were transformed,
As if the sense of love dissolved in them
Had folded itself round the spherèd world.
My vision then grew clear, and I could see
Into the mysteries of the universe:
Dizzy as with delight I floated down,
Winnowing the lightsome air with languid plumes,
My courses sought their birthplace in the sun,
Where they henceforth will live exempt from toil,
Pasturing flowers of vegetable fire;
And where my moonlike car will stand within
A temple, gazed upon by Phidian forms
Of thee, and Asia, and the Earth, and me,
And you fair nymphs looking the love we feel,—
In memory of the tidings it has borne,—
Beneath a dome fretted with graven flowers,
Poised on twelve columns of resplendent stone,
And open to the bright and liquid sky.
Yoked to it by an amphisbaenic snake
The likeness of those wingèd steeds will mock
The flight from which they find repose. Alas,

Whither has wandered now my partial tongue
When all remains untold which ye would hear?
As I have said, I floated to the earth:
It was, as it is still, the pain of bliss
To move, to breathe, to be; I wandering went
Among the haunts and dwellings of mankind,
And first was disappointed not to see
Such mighty change as I had felt within
Expressed in outward things; but soon I looked,
And behold, thrones were kingless, and men walked
One with the other even as spirits do,
None fawned, none trampled; hate, disdain, or fear,
Self-love or self-contempt, on human brows
No more inscribed, as o'er the gate of hell,
'All hope abandon ye who enter here;'
None frowned, none trembled, none with eager fear
Gazed on another's eye of cold command,
Until the subject of a tyrant's will
Became, worse fate, the abject of his own,
Which spurred him, like an outspent horse, to death.
None wrought his lips in truth-entangling lines
Which smiled the lie his tongue disdained to speak;
None, with firm sneer, trod out in his own heart
The sparks of love and hope till there remained
Those bitter ashes, a soul self-consumed,
And the wretch crept a vampire among men,
Infecting all with his own hideous ill;

None talked that common, false, cold, hollow talk
Which makes the heart deny the *yes* it breathes,
Yet question that unmeant hypocrisy
With such a self-mistrust as has no name.
And women, too, frank, beautiful, and kind
As the free heaven which rains fresh light and dew
On the wide earth, past; gentle radiant forms,
From custom's evil taint exempt and pure;
Speaking the wisdom once they could not think,
Looking emotions once they feared to feel,
And changed to all which once they dared not be,
Yet being now, made earth like heaven; nor pride,
Nor jealousy, nor envy, nor ill shame,
The bitterest of those drops of treasured gall,
Spoilt the sweet taste of the nepenthe, love.

Thrones, altars, judgement-seats, and prisons; wherein,
And beside which, by wretched men were borne
Sceptres, tiaras, swords, and chains, and tomes
Of reasoned wrong, glozed on by ignorance,
Were like those monstrous and barbaric shapes,
The ghosts of a no-more-remembered fame,
Which, from their unworn obelisks, look forth
In triumph o'er the palaces and tombs
Of those who were their conquerors: mouldering round,
These imaged to the pride of kings and priests
A dark yet mighty faith, a power as wide

As is the world it wasted, and are now
But an astonishment; even so the tools
And emblems of its last captivity,
Amid the dwellings of the peopled earth,
Stand, not o'erthrown, but unregarded now.
And those foul shapes, abhorred by god and man,—
Which, under many a name and many a form
Strange, savage, ghastly, dark and execrable,
Were Jupiter, the tyrant of the world;
And which the nations, panic-stricken, served
With blood, and hearts broken by long hope, and love
Dragged to his altars soiled and garlandless,
And slain amid men's unreclaiming tears,
Flattering the thing they feared, which fear was hate,—
Frown, mouldering fast, o'er their abandoned shrines:
The painted veil, by those who were, called life,
Which mimicked, as with colours idly spread,
All men believed or hoped, is torn aside;
The loathsome mask has fallen, the man remains
Sceptreless, free, uncircumscribed, but man
Equal, unclassed, tribeless, and nationless,
Exempt from awe, worship, degree, the king
Over himself; just, gentle, wise: but man
Passionless?—no, yet free from guilt or pain,
Which were, for his will made or suffered them,
Nor yet exempt, though ruling them like slaves,
From chance, and death, and mutability,

The clogs of that which else might oversoar
The loftiest star of unascended heaven,
Pinnacled dim in the intense inane.

THE TRIUMPH OF LIFE

Swift as a spirit hastening to his task
Of glory and of good, the Sun sprang forth
Rejoicing in his splendour, and the mask

Of darkness fell from the awakened Earth—
The smokeless altars of the mountain snows
Flamed above crimson clouds, and at the birth

Of light, the Ocean's orison arose,
To which the birds tempered their matin lay.
All flowers in field or forest which unclose

Their trembling eyelids to the kiss of day,
Swinging their censers in the element,
With orient incense lit by the new ray

Burned slow and inconsumably, and sent
Their odorous sighs up to the smiling air;
And, in succession due, did continent,

Isle, ocean, and all things that in them wear
The form and character of mortal mould,
Rise as the Sun their father rose, to bear

Their portion of the toil, which he of old
Took as his own, and then imposed on them:
But I, whom thoughts which must remain untold

Had kept as wakeful as the stars that gem
The cone of night, now they were laid asleep
Stretched my faint limbs beneath the hoary stem

Which an old chestnut flung athwart the steep
Of a green Apennine: before me fled
The night; behind me rose the day; the deep

Was at my feet, and Heaven above my head,—
When a strange trance over my fancy grew
Which was not slumber, for the shade it spread

Was so transparent, that the scene came through
As clear as when a veil of light is drawn
O'er evening hills they glimmer; and I knew

That I had felt the freshness of that dawn
Bathe in the same cold dew my brow and hair,
And sate as thus upon that slope of lawn

Under the self-same bough, and heard as there
The birds, the fountains and the ocean hold
Sweet talk in music through the enamoured air,
And then a vision on my brain was rolled.

As in that trance of wondrous thought I lay,
This was the tenour of my waking dream:—
Methought I sate beside a public way

Thick strewn with summer dust, and a great stream
Of people there was hurrying to and fro,
Numerous as gnats upon the evening gleam,

All hastening onward, yet none seemed to know
Whither he went, or whence he came, or why
He made one of the multitude, and so

Was borne amid the crowd, as through the sky
One of the million leaves of summer's bier;
Old age and youth, manhood and infancy,

Mixed in one mighty torrent did appear,
Some flying from the thing they feared, and some
Seeking the object of another's fear;

And others, as with steps towards the tomb,
Pored on the trodden worms that crawled beneath,
And others mournfully within the gloom

Of their own shadow walked, and called it death;
And some fled from it as it were a ghost,
Half fainting in the affliction of vain breath:

But more, with motions which each other crossed,
Pursued or shunned the shadows the clouds threw,
Or birds within the noonday aether lost,

Upon that path where flowers never grew,—
And, weary with vain toil and faint for thirst,
Heard not the fountains, whose melodious dew

Out of their mossy cells forever burst;
Nor felt the breeze which from the forest told
Of grassy paths and wood-lawns interspersed

With overarching elms and caverns cold,
And violet banks where sweet dreams brood, but they
Pursued their serious folly as of old.

And as I gazed, methought that in the way
The throng grew wilder, as the woods of June
When the south wind shakes the extinguished day,

And a cold glare, intenser than the noon,
But icy cold, obscured with blinding light
The sun, as he the stars. Like the young moon—

When on the sunlit limits of the night
Her white shell trembles amid crimson air,
And whilst the sleeping tempest gathers might—

Doth, as the herald of its coming, bear
The ghost of its dead mother, whose dim form
Bends in dark aether from her infant's chair,—

So came a chariot on the silent storm
Of its own rushing splendour, and a Shape
So sate within, as one whom years deform,

Beneath a dusky hood and double cape,
Crouching within the shadow of a tomb;
And o'er what seemed the head a cloud-like crape

Was bent, a dun and faint aethereal gloom
Tempering the light. Upon the chariot-beam
A Janus-visaged Shadow did assume

The guidance of that wonder-wingèd team;
The shapes which drew it in thick lightenings
Were lost:—I heard alone on the air's soft stream

The music of their ever-moving wings.
All the four faces of that Charioteer
Had their eyes banded; little profit brings

Speed in the van and blindness in the rear,
Nor then avail the beams that quench the sun,—
Or that with banded eyes could pierce the sphere

Of all that is, has been or will be done;
So ill was the car guided—but it passed
With solemn speed majestically on.

The crowd gave way, and I arose aghast,
Or seemed to rise, so mighty was the trance,
And saw, like clouds upon the thunder-blast,

The million with fierce song and maniac dance
Raging around—such seemed the jubilee
As when to greet some conqueror's advance

Imperial Rome poured forth her living sea
From senate-house, and forum, and theatre,
When   upon the free

Had bound a yoke, which soon they stooped to bear.
Nor wanted here the just similitude
Of a triumphal pageant, for where'er

The chariot rolled, a captive multitude
Was driven;—all those who had grown old in power
Or misery,—all who had their age subdued

By action or by suffering, and whose hour
Was drained to its last sand in weal or woe,
So that the trunk survived both fruit and flower;—

All those whose fame or infamy must grow
Till the great winter lay the form and name
Of this green earth with them for ever low;—

All but the sacred few who could not tame
Their spirits to the conquerors—but as soon
As they had touched the world with living flame,

Fled back like eagles to their native noon,
Or those who put aside the diadem
Of earthly thrones or gems . . .

Were there, of Athens or Jerusalem,
Were neither mid the mighty captives seen,
Nor mid the ribald crowd that followed them,

Nor those who went before fierce and obscene.
The wild dance maddens in the van, and those
Who lead it—fleet as shadows on the green,

Outspeed the chariot, and without repose
Mix with each other in tempestuous measure
To savage music, wilder as it grows,

They, tortured by their agonizing pleasure,
Convulsed and on the rapid whirlwinds spun
Of that fierce Spirit, whose unholy leisure

Was soothed by mischief since the world begun,
Throw back their heads and loose their streaming hair;
And in their dance round her who dims the sun,

Maidens and youths fling their wild arms in air
As their feet twinkle; they recede, and now
Bending within each other's atmosphere,

Kindle invisibly—and as they glow,
Like moths by light attracted and repelled,
Oft to their bright destruction come and go,

Till like two clouds into one vale impelled,
That shake the mountains when their lightnings mingle
And die in rain—the fiery band which held

Their natures, snaps—while the shock still may tingle;
One falls and then another in the path
Senseless—nor is the desolation single,

Yet ere I can say *where*—the chariot hath
Passed over them—nor other trace I find
But as of foam after the ocean's wrath

Is spent upon the desert shore;—behind,
Old men and women foully disarrayed,
Shake their gray hairs in the insulting wind,

And follow in the dance, with limbs decayed,
Seeking to reach the light which leaves them still
Farther behind and deeper in the shade.

But not the less with impotence of will
They wheel, though ghastly shadows interpose
Round them and round each other, and fulfil

Their work, and in the dust from whence they rose
Sink, and corruption veils them as they lie,
And past in these performs what   in those.

Struck to the heart by this sad pageantry,
Half to myself I said—'And what is this?
Whose shape is that within the car? And why—'

I would have added—'is all here amiss?—'
But a voice answered—'Life!'—I turned, and knew
(O Heaven, have mercy on such wretchedness!)

That what I thought was an old root which grew
To strange distortion out of the hill side,
Was indeed one of those deluded crew,

And that the grass, which methought hung so wide
And white, was but his thin discoloured hair,
And that the holes he vainly sought to hide,

Were or had been eyes:—'If thou canst, forbear
To join the dance, which I had well forborne!'
Said the grim Feature (of my thought aware).

'I will unfold that which to this deep scorn
Led me and my companions, and relate
The progress of the pageant since the morn;

'If thirst of knowledge shall not then abate,
Follow it thou even to the night, but I
Am weary.'—Then like one who with the weight

Of his own words is staggered, wearily
He paused; and ere he could resume, I cried:
'First, who art thou?'—'Before thy memory,

'I feared, loved, hated, suffered, did and died,
And if the spark with which Heaven lit my spirit
Had been with purer nutriment supplied,

'Corruption would not now thus much inherit
Of what was once Rousseau,—nor this disguise
Stain that which ought to have disdained to wear it;

'If I have been extinguished, yet there rise
A thousand beacons from the spark I bore'—
'And who are those chained to the car?'—'The wise,

'The great, the unforgotten,—they who wore
Mitres and helms and crowns, or wreaths of light,
Signs of thought's empire over thought—their lore

'Taught them not this, to know themselves; their might
Could not repress the mystery within,
And for the morn of truth they feigned, deep night

'Caught them ere evening.'—'Who is he with chin
Upon his breast, and hands crossed on his chain?'—
'The child of a fierce hour; he sought to win

'The world, and lost all that it did contain
Of greatness, in its hope destroyed; and more
Of fame and peace than virtue's self can gain

'Without the opportunity which bore
Him on its eagle pinions to the peak
From which a thousand climbers have before

'Fallen, as Napoleon fell.'—I felt my cheek
Alter, to see the shadow pass away,
Whose grasp had left the giant world so weak

That every pigmy kicked it as it lay;
And much I grieved to think how power and will
In opposition rule our mortal day,

And why God made irreconcilable
Good and the means of good; and for despair
I half disdained mine eyes' desire to fill

With the spent vision of the times that were
And scarce have ceased to be.—'Dost thou behold,'
Said my guide, 'those spoilers spoiled, Voltaire,

'Frederick, and Paul, Catherine, and Leopold,
And hoary anarchs, demagogues, and sage—
     names which the world thinks always old,

'For in the battle Life and they did wage,
She remained conqueror. I was overcome
By my own heart alone, which neither age,

'Nor tears, nor infamy, nor now the tomb
Could temper to its object.'—'Let them pass,'
I cried, 'the world and its mysterious doom

'Is not so much more glorious than it was,
That I desire to worship those who drew
New figures on its false and fragile glass

'As the old faded.'—'Figures ever new
Rise on the bubble, paint them as you may;
We have but thrown, as those before us threw,

'Our shadows on it as it passed away.
But mark how chained to the triumphal chair
The mighty phantoms of an elder day;

'All that is mortal of great Plato there
Expiates the joy and woe his master knew not;
The star that ruled his doom was far too fair,

'And life, where long that flower of Heaven grew not,
Conquered that heart by love, which gold, or pain,
Or age, or sloth, or slavery could subdue not.

'And near him walk the   twain,
The tutor and his pupil, whom Dominion
Followed as tame as vulture in a chain.

'The world was darkened beneath either pinion
Of him whom from the flock of conquerors
Fame singled out for her thunder-bearing minion;

'The other long outlived both woes and wars,
Throned in the thoughts of men, and still had kept
The jealous key of Truth's eternal doors,

'If Bacon's eagle spirit had not lept
Like lightning out of darkness—he compelled
The Proteus shape of Nature, as it slept

'To wake, and lead him to the caves that held
The treasure of the secrets of its reign.
See the great bards of elder time, who quelled

'The passions which they sung, as by their strain
May well be known: their living melody
Tempers its own contagion to the vein

'Of those who are infected with it—I
Have suffered what I wrote, or viler pain!
And so my words have seeds of misery—

'Even as the deeds of others, not as theirs.'
And then he pointed to a company,

'Midst whom I quickly recognized the heirs
Of Caesar's crime, from him to Constantine;
The anarch chiefs, whose force and murderous snares

Had founded many a sceptre-bearing line,
And spread the plague of gold and blood abroad:
And Gregory and John, and men divine,

Who rose like shadows between man and God;
Till that eclipse, still hanging over heaven,
Was worshipped by the world o'er which they strode,

For the true sun it quenched—'Their power was given
But to destroy,' replied the leader:—'I
Am one of those who have created, even

'If it be but a world of agony.'—
'Whence camest thou? and whither goest thou?
How did thy course begin?' I said, 'and why?

'Mine eyes are sick of this perpetual flow
Of people, and my heart sick of one sad thought—
Speak!'—'Whence I am, I partly seem to know,

'And how and by what paths I have been brought
To this dread pass, methinks even thou mayst guess;—
Why this should be, my mind can compass not;

'Whither the conqueror hurries me, still less;—
But follow thou, and from spectator turn
Actor or victim in this wretchedness,

'And what thou wouldst be taught I then may learn
From thee. Now listen:—In the April prime,
When all the forest-tips began to burn

'With kindling green, touched by the azure clime
Of the young season, I was laid asleep
Under a mountain, which from unknown time

'Had yawned into a cavern, high and deep;
And from it came a gentle rivulet,
Whose water, like clear air, in its calm sweep

'Bent the soft grass, and kept for ever wet
The stems of the sweet flowers, and filled the grove
With sounds, which whoso hears must needs forget

'All pleasure and all pain, all hate and love,
Which they had known before that hour of rest;
A sleeping mother then would dream not of

'Her only child who died upon the breast
At eventide—a king would mourn no more
The crown of which his brows were dispossessed

'When the sun lingered o'er his ocean floor
To gild his rival's new prosperity.
Thou wouldst forget thus vainly to deplore

'Ills, which if ills can find no cure from thee,
The thought of which no other sleep will quell,
Nor other music blot from memory,

'So sweet and deep is the oblivious spell;
And whether life had been before that sleep
The Heaven which I imagine, or a Hell

'Like this harsh world in which I wake to weep,
I know not. I arose, and for a space
The scene of woods and waters seemed to keep,

'Though it was now broad day, a gentle trace
Of light diviner than the common sun
Sheds on the common earth, and all the place

'Was filled with magic sounds woven into one
Oblivious melody, confusing sense
Amid the gliding waves and shadows dun;

'And, as I looked, the bright omnipresence
Of morning through the orient cavern flowed,
And the sun's image radiantly intense

'Burned on the waters of the well that glowed
Like gold, and threaded all the forest's maze
With winding paths of emerald fire; there stood

'Amid the sun, as he amid the blaze
Of his own glory, on the vibrating
Floor of the fountain, paved with flashing rays,

'A Shape all light, which with one hand did fling
Dew on the earth, as if she were the dawn,
And the invisible rain did ever sing

'A silver music on the mossy lawn;
And still before me on the dusky grass,
Iris her many-coloured scarf had drawn:

'In her right hand she bore a crystal glass,
Mantling with bright Nepenthe; the fierce splendour
Fell from her as she moved under the mass

'Of the deep cavern, and with palms so tender,
Their tread broke not the mirror of its billow,
Glided along the river, and did bend her

'Head under the dark boughs, till like a willow
Her fair hair swept the bosom of the stream
That whispered with delight to be its pillow.

'As one enamoured is upborne in dream
O'er lily-paven lakes, mid silver mist,
To wondrous music, so this shape might seem

'Partly to tread the waves with feet which kissed
The dancing foam; partly to glide along
The air which roughened the moist amethyst,

'Or the faint morning beams that fell among
The trees, or the soft shadows of the trees;
And her feet, ever to the ceaseless song

'Of leaves, and winds, and waves, and birds, and bees,
And falling drops, moved in a measure new
Yet sweet, as on the summer evening breeze,

'Up from the lake a shape of golden dew
Between two rocks, athwart the rising moon,
Dances i' the wind, where never eagle flew;

'And still her feet, no less than the sweet tune
To which they moved, seemed as they moved to blot
The thoughts of him who gazed on them; and soon

'All that was, seemed as if it had been not;
And all the gazer's mind was strewn beneath
Her feet like embers; and she, thought by thought,

'Trampled its sparks into the dust of death;
As day upon the threshold of the east
Treads out the lamps of night, until the breath

'Of darkness re-illumine even the least
Of heaven's living eyes—like day she came,
Making the night a dream; and ere she ceased

'To move, as one between desire and shame
Suspended, I said—If, as it doth seem,
Thou comest from the realm without a name

'Into this valley of perpetual dream,
Show whence I came, and where I am, and why—
Pass not away upon the passing stream.

'Arise and quench thy thirst, was her reply.
And as a shut lily stricken by the wand
Of dewy morning's vital alchemy,

'I rose; and, bending at her sweet command,
Touched with faint lips the cup she raised,
And suddenly my brain became as sand

'Where the first wave had more than half erased
The track of deer on desert Labrador;
Whilst the wolf, from which they fled amazed,

'Leaves his stamp visibly upon the shore,
Until the second bursts;—so on my sight
Burst a new vision, never seen before,

'And the fair shape waned in the coming light,
As veil by veil the silent splendour drops
From Lucifer, amid the chrysolite

'Of sunrise, ere it tinge the mountain-tops;
And as the presence of that fairest planet,
Although unseen, is felt by one who hopes

'That his day's path may end as he began it,
In that star's smile, whose light is like the scent
Of a jonquil when evening breezes fan it,

'Or the soft note in which his dear lament
The Brescian shepherd breathes, or the caress
That turned his weary slumber to content;

'So knew I in that light's severe excess
The presence of that Shape which on the stream
Moved, as I moved along the wilderness,

'More dimly than a day-appearing dream,
The ghost of a forgotten form of sleep;
A light of heaven, whose half-extinguished beam

'Through the sick day in which we wake to weep
Glimmers, for ever sought, for ever lost;
So did that shape its obscure tenour keep

'Beside my path, as silent as a ghost;
But the new Vision, and the cold bright car,
With solemn speed and stunning music, crossed

'The forest, and as if from some dread war
Triumphantly returning, the loud million
Fiercely extolled the fortune of her star.

'A moving arch of victory, the vermilion
And green and azure plumes of Iris had
Built high over her wind-wingèd pavilion,

'And underneath aethereal glory clad
The wilderness, and far before her flew
The tempest of the splendour, which forbade

'Shadow to fall from leaf and stone; the crew
Seemed in that light, like atomies to dance
Within a sunbeam;—some upon the new

'Embroidery of flowers, that did enhance
The grassy vesture of the desert, played,
Forgetful of the chariot's swift advance;

'Others stood gazing, till within the shade
Of the great mountain its light left them dim;
Others outspeeded it; and others made

'Circles around it, like the clouds that swim
Round the high moon in a bright sea of air;
And more did follow, with exulting hymn,

'The chariot and the captives fettered there:—
But all like bubbles on an eddying flood
Fell into the same track at last, and were

'Borne onward.—I among the multitude
Was swept—me, sweetest flowers delayed not long;
Me, not the shadow nor the solitude;

'Me, not that falling stream's Lethean song;
Me, not the phantom of that early Form
Which moved upon its motion—but among

'The thickest billows of that living storm
I plunged, and bared my bosom to the clime
Of that cold light, whose airs too soon deform.

'Before the chariot had begun to climb
The opposing steep of that mysterious dell,
Behold a wonder worthy of the rhyme

'Of him who from the lowest depths of hell,
Through every paradise and through all glory,
Love led serene, and who returned to tell

'The words of hate and awe; the wondrous story
How all things are transfigured except Love;
For deaf as is a sea, which wrath makes hoary,

'The world can hear not the sweet notes that move
The sphere whose light is melody to lovers—
A wonder worthy of his rhyme.—The grove

'Grew dense with shadows to its inmost covers,
The earth was gray with phantoms, and the air
Was peopled with dim forms, as when there hovers

'A flock of vampire-bats before the glare
Of the tropic sun, bringing, ere evening,
Strange night upon some Indian isle;—thus were

'Phantoms diffused around; and some did fling
Shadows of shadows, yet unlike themselves,
Behind them; some like eaglets on the wing

'Were lost in the white day; others like elves
Danced in a thousand unimagined shapes
Upon the sunny streams and grassy shelves;

'And others sate chattering like restless apes
On vulgar hands, . . .
Some made a cradle of the ermined capes

'Of kingly mantles; some across the tiar
Of pontiffs sate like vultures; others played
Under the crown which girt with empire

'A baby's or an idiot's brow, and made
Their nests in it. The old anatomies
Sate hatching their bare broods under the shade

'Of daemon wings, and laughed from their dead eyes
To reassume the delegated power,
Arrayed in which those worms did monarchize,

'Who made this earth their charnel. Others more
Humble, like falcons, sate upon the fist
Of common men, and round their heads did soar;

'Or like small gnats and flies, as thick as mist
On evening marshes, thronged about the brow
Of lawyers, statesmen, priest and theorist;—

'And others, like discoloured flakes of snow
On fairest bosoms and the sunniest hair,
Fell, and were melted by the youthful glow

'Which they extinguished; and, like tears, they were
A veil to those from whose faint lids they rained
In drops of sorrow. I became aware

'Of whence those forms preceeded which thus stained
The track in which we moved. After brief space,
From every form the beauty slowly waned;

'From every firmest limb and fairest face
The strength and freshness fell like dust, and left
The action and the shape without the grace

246

'Of life. The marble brow of youth was cleft
With care; and in those eyes where once hope shone,
Desire, like a lioness bereft

'Of her last cub, glared ere it died; each one
Of that great crowd sent forth incessantly
These shadows, numerous as the dead leaves blown

'In autumn evening from a poplar tree.
Each like himself and like each other were
At first; but some distorted seemed to be

'Obscure clouds, moulded by the casual air;
And of this stuff the car's creative ray
Wrought all the busy phantoms that were there,

'As the sun shapes the clouds; thus on the way
Mask after mask fell from the countenance
And form of all; and long before the day

'Was old, the joy which waked like heaven's glance
The sleepers in the oblivious valley, died;
And some grew weary of the ghastly dance,

'And fell, as I have fallen, by the wayside;—
Those soonest from whose forms most shadows passed,
And least of strength and beauty did abide.

'Then, what is life? I cried.'—   247

INDEX OF FIRST LINES